T5-AQS-798

School Crisis Management Manual

Judie Smith

School Crisis Management Manual

Guidelines for Administrators

Judie Smith

L̶P LEARNING PUBLICATIONS, INC.
Holmes Beach, Florida

ISBN 1-55691-127-0

© 1997 by Judie Smith

All rights reserved. No part of this book may be reproduced or transmitted in any form or by any means, electronic or mechanical, including photocopying and recording, or by any information or retrieval systems, without permission in writing from the publisher.

Learning Publications, Inc.
5351 Gulf Drive
P.O. Box 1338
Holmes Beach, FL 34218-1338

Printing: 5 4 3 2   Year: 10 9

Printed in the United States of America.

Contents

Suggested Goals and Objectives of a School Crisis Management System • **Levels of Crises:**
Level 1—An Individual Tragedy or Event • Level 2—A Major Crisis Impacting a Single School
• Level 3—Disaster Affecting One or More Schools

Part 1: Preparation

Selecting a School Crisis Team • **Responsibilities of Campus Crisis Team Members:** The
Principal or Team Leader • The Nurse • The Counselor, School Social Worker, and the School
Psychologist • The Security Officer • The Parent Liaison • The Faculty Liaison • **Training a
Campus Crisis Team:** Sample Training Agenda • Pre-training Questionnaire • **Sample Crisis
Scenarios:** Elementary School • Secondary School

Developing a School Crisis Plan • **Targets and Strategies:** Target 1—To Establish a Campus
Crisis Team • Target 2—To Have a Prepared Plan for Sharing Information during a Crisis •
Target 3—To Prepare School Personnel to Respond Effectively to Crises • Target 4—To Use
the Building in an Efficient Manner in the Event of a Crisis • Target 5—To Make Provisions for
Special Populations • Target 6—To Use Community Resources to Prevent and Resolve Crises in
Schools • Target 7—To Maintain a Safe Environment for Students and Staff • **School Safety
Suggestions** • **School Crisis Plan Review and Evaluation**

An Emergency Management Exercise • Observation Checklist • **Sample Crisis Drill
Scenarios:** Exercise 1—An Angry Student with a Gun in Secondary School • Exercise 2—The
Arrest of an Elementary School Teacher • Exercise 3—The Death of an Elementary School
Teacher • Exercise 4—The Suicide of a Secondary School Student

Part 2: Intervention

Communication • The Media • Twenty-nine Crisis Situations

Part 3: Resolution

Introduction

The need for crisis management in schools is a relatively recent phenomenon. A spitball shot at the teacher or a couple of kids playing hooky used to bring swift discipline and a bad mark on the citizenship or deportment section of the report card. Few middle-aged parents can remember a teenage friend committing suicide, gangs were restricted to the inner-city ghetto, and child abuse was unrecognized. Accidents and illness may have caused an untimely death but the schools rarely saw a need to offer grief counseling. Vandalism and theft worried administrators but it never occurred to anyone that a school may be the target of terrorism or an intruder who would do harm to a child. Drugs, sex, and violence were unusual topics for films or literature and banned from library shelves or theaters.

The social upheavals in the last decade have seen a dramatic change in the concerns for the safety of school children. A visitor to a school building today might be amazed to watch the students enter through a metal detector and submit their book bags for a daily search. While security measures are effective, a school crisis does occur on or off campus all too often despite the tremendous efforts being made to protect students and staff. Safety is high on the priority list of most school districts' goals. The following incident demonstrates a reason for these new concerns.

A middle-school student in Dallas, Texas, was suspended from school for serious violation of school rules. A few days later, the disgruntled boy tried to enter the building but was recognized by a security guard and, bypassing the walk-through metal detector, was taken immediately to the security office. There he pulled out a gun, ran out of the office, and up the stairs to the third floor with classes in session. He walked the hall, periodically opening classroom doors, waving the gun, and shouting obscenities. The terrorized students essentially were held hostage for several hours while the rest of the building was evacuated according to their crisis plan and the police SWAT team prevented a serious tragedy. Fortunately the boy surrendered without physically hurting anyone but the emotional turmoil lingered many days. The campus and district crisis teams organized an extensive counseling effort to assist the school and community in resolving their feelings of anger and fear.

Across the country, such crises impel school districts to draft action plans to address a disturbing escalation in campus emergencies. By diminishing chaos and panic, disseminating accurate information, attending to the emotional strain on staff and students, and providing essential follow-up services, such plans can and do greatly relieve the burdens placed upon principals and other school personnel. Schools are no longer the safe haven they used to be and school administrators realize the need to prepare themselves to meet challenges such as the middle-school principal faced in Dallas.

This manual is intended to be a resource for those responsible for the development of school crisis plans. The suggestions stem from over 10 years of experience working with schools in preparing crisis plans, coordinating crisis counseling services and helping schools resolve the emotional aftermath following traumatic experiences.

The manual is divided into three sections. **Part 1** deals with preparation. Careful planning often prevents the escalation of a crisis and eases the chaos that so often accompanies such an emergency. The content in this section focuses on selecting and training a crisis team and includes an outline that can be used for writing a crisis plan. Each school must develop a specific plan suiting their own needs and each plan should include a team of trained individuals who are prepared to respond if and when a crisis does occur.

Part 2 provides step-by-step guidelines for managing a variety of crisis situations. It includes the mitigation of and immediate response to an emergency. There are similar aspects for all crises such as a need for communication and rumor control. But some crises require additional planning such as dealing with a bomb threat when a principal must make critical decisions whether the threat is a hoax or life threatening.

The third and final section addresses issues that arise during the resolution phase of a crisis. Once the emergency has subsided the crisis may still create issues that cannot be ignored. Recovery begins with stress management for the crisis workers in the debriefing, after-action review. Suggestions for conducting parent meetings for an upset community are included in **Part 3**.

Suggested Goals and Objectives of a School Crisis Management System

Goals

- To increase the security of the staff and students.

- To minimize the damage and loss.

- To return the school to its normal functioning level as soon as possible by diminishing the chaos and confusion.

- To provide the necessary counseling to assist students and staff, who are emotionally affected by the crisis, to deal with the trauma.

Objectives

- To outline a predetermined plan of action which may be used to respond to emergencies or disasters.

- To establish small groups of specifically selected and trained individuals who collectively have the knowledge, skills, and sensitivity to act as crisis management specialists.

- To develop an information sharing system to contain rumors and prevent escalation of the crisis.

- To utilize community resources and create a partnership with parents following crisis events.

- To provide guidelines for responding to the media during a crisis.

- To outline stress management and debriefing procedures for crisis workers.

Levels of Crises

A crisis is defined as a critical situation that creates an emotional impact on those involved and has the potential of changing a person's life. It is not the situation itself but how people feel and react to it or the psychological reaction to the threat that makes it a crisis. An overwhelming intensity of emotions (fear, anger, sadness) interferes with the ability to think clearly and make sound decisions. Cognitive skills diminish. A crisis is unique: What affects one person may not affect another as drastically. A crisis is time limited: The immediate and severe psychological reactions will pass with time. What concerns schools is not only the short-term explosive turmoil but the possibility of the longer lasting effect post-traumatic stress may have on the mental well- being of the students.

Following a crisis, depending on how the threat of danger is handled, there is opportunity for growth. Emotional maturity comes from learning how to cope with sudden and devastating adversities. The Chinese symbol for crisis means danger and opportunity.

The framework of a comprehensive crisis management system outlines the involvement of key personnel according to the nature, scope, and intensity of crises. Crisis events can be divided into three levels depending on the impact of the event. Thus, minor, localized crises would involve only local school personnel while major crises or catastrophes might activate personnel at the school site plus additional district and community services.

Any of the following examples has the potential of escalating to a more serious level if the impact is unusually severe or does not require a full scale crisis management effort if the impact is less severe than usual. For example, the death of a student who recently enrolled or had not often attended classes and is not well-known may not trigger a large group of grieving students and teachers. It is possible that the crisis could be classified as a Level 1 crisis instead of Level 2.

Level 1: An Individual Tragedy or Event

A Level 1 crisis involves a personal tragedy and threatening incidents primarily affecting a student, teacher, or administrator and impacting a single school.

Such incidents would possibly involve:

- Local school crisis team

- School security

- Additional school mental health personnel assigned to the school

Examples:

- Death of a parent, guardian, or significant family member

- Suicide threat (high risk)

- Suicide attempt off campus

- Contagious disease

- Violent or bizarre behavior of a student

- Dangerous or irate person on campus

- Serious illness of a student or faculty member

- Assault of a student on campus

- Evidence of suspected cult activity

- Community or political protest activity

- Bomb threat

- Child abuse or neglect

- Weapons on campus

Level 2: A Major Crisis Impacting a Single School

Level 2 constitutes a major personal crisis or threatening incident at a single school or major disaster elsewhere that indirectly impacts students and teachers.

Such incidents would possibly involve:

- Local school crisis team

- School security

- Additional school mental health personnel assigned to the school

- Additional district administrators

- Additional district crisis management specialists

- Community mental health personnel

- Community emergency services

- News media

Examples:

- Accusation against school personnel involved in illegal activities such as child abuse or molestation

- Death of a teacher or student off campus

- National incident or declaration of war

- Undercover police work disclosed

- School bus accident with several severe injuries

- Suicide attempt at school

- Altercation or violence between groups or gang members

- Abduction

Level 3: Disaster Affecting One or More Schools

A Level 3 crisis involves terrorism, disaster, or threatened disaster that directly and profoundly affects one or more schools.

Such incidents would possibly involve:

- Local school crisis team

- School security

- Additional mental health personnel temporarily assigned to the school

- Additional district administrators

- Additional district crisis management specialists

- Community mental health personnel

- Community emergency services

- News media

Examples:

- Tornado, severe windstorm, flood

- Taking of hostages or sniper gunfire

- Air crash, explosion, fire

- Cluster suicides

- Death at school

- Environmental hazard, chemical spill

Part 1
Preparation

School Crisis Team

Selecting a School Crisis Team

Each school should have a team of trained personnel in place and ready to respond to a variety of crisis situations. The team is responsible for following a plan of action that would help ensure the safety of the students and staff and return the school to its normal routine as soon as possible. Larger school districts may have a districtwide team of crisis management experts that would assist, but the local team would need to respond immediately if the crisis occurred on campus during school hours and continue to offer follow-up services after the district team and community assistance leaves the campus.

The team may be assigned the following tasks:

- To learn about crisis management by attending training sessions

- To develop a crisis plan for the school including a needs assessment

- To provide an orientation for the faculty

- To inform the community and the school district's central administration of the crisis plan

- To practice their role during a drill

- To carry out their responsibilities during an actual crisis

- To review and revise the crisis plan on an annual basis

The members of this team are carefully selected for the role they will play during and after a crisis.

Some characteristics to consider when selecting crisis team members:

- Ability to handle stress with a minimum of other stressors present in their personal lives

- Ability to remain calm when others are upset and emotional

- Ability to make good decisions in emergency situations

- Ability to follow instructions and work well with a team

- Flexibility

- A willingness to accept responsibility

- Familiarity of the community

- Knowledgeable about the functioning and organization of the school

The principal should select the team members with these qualities in mind but also allow a staff person to have the option of choosing not to serve on the team. Each member needs to be a willing part of the team or resentment could jeopardize the smooth functioning during crisis response.

The size of the team varies with the size of the school facility and student body. Six or seven people usually are sufficient if the school district has a districtwide team or nearby schools could supplement additional crisis counselors if needed for a major problem. The whole team may not be called into action for every crisis event.

The nature of the crisis would determine which of the team members would be called away from their regular daily assignment to help on an emergency basis. For example, a dangerous intruder in the building primarily would call for team members responsible for security. Those team members who are skilled crisis counselors may be needed after the death of a student who had been hospitalized for some time. If a student is murdered and there is a threat of retaliation, both security and counseling may be appropriate.

Availability is always a concern. The very nature of a crisis is that is unexpected. Each team member must be able to set aside other duties and responsibilities to join the crisis team as quickly as possible. They must have advanced permission from their supervisors to drop other assignments immediately and follow the directions of the crisis team leader or coordinator. A well-prepared school team can gather within minutes. A well-prepared district team can arrive at the school within an hour.

Responsibilities of Campus Crisis Team Members

Although each school would consider their own needs and personnel available, some general roles and responsibilities of crisis team members can be delineated.

The Principal or Team Leader's Responsibilities

- Assume responsibility for all decisions made and actions taken

- Verify the crisis situation

- Notify emergency services

- Assess the situation and determine what actions are needed

- Convene the campus crisis team

- Direct the crisis team to provide for:

  - protection and evacuation

  - medical attention

  - information sharing with staff, students, and parents

  - counseling

- Brief the district's central administration

- Conduct a faculty meeting

- Arrange for substitute teachers

- Serve as a spokesperson to the media

- Call on community resources for assistance

- Chair parent meetings

- Reassess the situation with the crisis team

- Debrief with the crisis team and evaluate the school's crisis management actions

- Continue intervention and follow-up or terminate crisis management services

- Document decisions

- Revise the school's crisis plan

The Nurse's Responsibilities:

- Administer first aid

- Request that paramedics and an ambulance be called

- Appoint someone to meet paramedics at the school's entrance and give direction to the location of the injured

- Brief the paramedics upon arrival and indicate which students are most seriously injured

- Arrange for someone to travel with students to the hospital

- Complete a referral form to accompany any injured student to be moved

- Call for additional school nursing assistance as needed

- Ask for clinic coverage by a principal's designate if the nurse is needed elsewhere

The Counselor, School Social Worker, and School Psychologist's Responsibilities:

- Arrange for counseling rooms

- Triage students to individual or group counseling

- Check on all students identified as vulnerable or deeply affected

- Provide individual counseling

- Facilitate support groups

- Visit classrooms

- Meet teachers informally and in groups

- Make home visits, deliver sympathy cards or donations

- Attend the funeral(s) or memorial(s)

- Monitor students' adjustment

- Coordinate re-entry plans for hospitalized students

- Provide follow-up support or counseling

- Consult with a resource person regarding cultural differences

The Security Officer's Responsibilities:

- Coordinate immediate security and protection

- Communicate with and assist the police and fire departments

- Act as a liaison with the juvenile and probation department

The Parent Liaison Responsibilities:

- Prepare a fact sheet for the secretary

- Answer telephone inquiries

- Draft a letter for students to take home to parents

- Facilitate the release of students to parents or guardians

- Relay injury reports from the nurse to parents

- Coordinate parent meetings

The Faculty Liaison Responsibilities:

- Keep the faculty informed

- Relay faculty needs to the principal

- Coordinate donations or assistance from the staff to the family or families

- Attend parent meetings

Training a Campus Crisis Team

Advanced planning is critical. The first step in preparation is to train the response personnel. When a team has been selected by the principal, team members will be responsible for devising a crisis plan for their school and for preparing themselves to fulfill their assigned responsibilities. As school safety needs and personnel change, the written crisis plan will need to be reviewed and additional training scheduled.

The tendency is for schools to organize and train a team, develop a crisis response plan, then consider the task to be complete. It is highly recommended to review and revise these plans on an annual basis. Unfortunately it may take a school's real emergency and trying to implement an outdated crisis plan to realize changes in the school and personnel have not been taken into account.

Crisis team training can be facilitated by an expert crisis management specialist or carefully planned by the school administrator. Each school must decide what fits its own needs best and what resources are available within the community or the district. Whoever plans the training must have knowledge about the school's setting and organization as well as crisis management issues. Mental health agencies, hospitals, law enforcement personnel, and the religious community may be called upon to present information about specific crisis topics such as grief, evacuation, violence, gangs, suicide, and child abuse, but always include a co-trainer who also knows the school system.

Sample Training Agenda

- **Introduction and Need for Pre-Crisis Planning**

  - Examples of safety concerns and past crisis events at the school or another school in the district

  - Video: *School Crisis Under Control* by the National School Safety Center, or *Crisis Management and Intervention,* seminar two, the Safe Schools and Communities Satellite Seminar Series, by the National Telelearning Network

- ◆ Objectives of training: to develop a written crisis plan and learn roles and responsibilities as a team member

■ **Pre-training questionnaire**

- ◆ Stimulate discussion and begin an outline for the crisis plan

■ **Identify existing school or district crisis management procedures and additional community resources**

■ **Team assignments:**

- ◆ Let participants brainstorm what specific responsibilities would be included and use suggestions from the section on Responsibilities of Team Members

■ **Crisis scenario exercise (use the examples on pages 13–14 or write a new one)**

■ **Preparation for future meetings**

- ◆ Set a meeting time and place

- ◆ Assign sections of written crisis plan

- ◆ Plan a crisis drill

- ◆ Prepare a faculty orientation

- ◆ Address specific crisis topics: grief, gangs, child abuse, violence, suicide, etc.

Pre-Training Questionnaire

Most people have a natural interest in safety and crisis issues. The news media relates daily stories of how innocent people are caught in emergency situations, tragic accidents cut lives short, and violence affects even our children. It is easy to identify with the victims in these stories. Anxiety is always increased on a school campus when vandals damage a car in the teachers' parking lot or an angry parent creates a ruckus in the principal's office. It is usually not as difficult to capture the interest of participants in a crisis management training as it is to focus their attention toward developing an actual crisis plan to get beyond the storytelling of personal experiences. The trainers can be prepared with a written questionnaire to help guide the task at hand.

The following suggested questions usually stimulate thought and discussion.

- What warning system is used in your school to signal a crisis?

- Where is an up-to-date floor plan and room assignment list kept for your school?

- What are the guidelines for granting interviews with the media during a crisis?

- What provisions have been made to accommodate handicapped students during a crisis?

- What suicide prevention measures are in place in your building?

- What system will be used to reunite students with parents if an evacuation of the school is necessary?

- What is the proper reporting procedure if you suspect child abuse?

- Who should be contacted in case of a major crisis on your campus?

- What major points should be included on a fact sheet following the homicide of a student and to whom should this information be given?

- What is the purpose of a debriefing following a crisis?

Sample Crisis Scenarios

Elementary School

An irate, disheveled father entered the school building by a side door at 9:30 a.m. Without stopping at the office he proceeded down the hall toward his 10-year-old son's classroom. A cafeteria worker observed his strange manner and notified the office. The principal quickly responded and recognized the father as he searched for the classroom. She was aware the mother had custody of the boy and there had been a restraining order against the father after several threats had been made. The principal confronted him before he found the classroom but he pushed her aside and burst into the room brandishing a gun at the teacher. He grabbed the frightened child and pointed the gun at his head yelling that if anyone tried to stop him he would kill the boy. Hearing the commotion, several teachers and other children ran into the hall and witnessed the father dragging the boy to his car. Many children in the classroom became hysterical. One little girl cowered in the corner and two boys ran out the exit door and headed for home. The teacher was visibly shaken and had difficulty speaking coherently.

Questions:

- What decisions need to be made and in what order?

- What responsibilities need to be delegated and to whom?

- What are the immediate and long-term needs of the children who were in the classroom and of the staff who witnessed the kidnapping?

- What information needs to be shared with whom and how?

- What additional assistance is needed from other resources or from community emergency assistance?

- What points need to be covered in a debriefing session with those who helped with the crisis management?

Secondary School

A car screeched by the black top at the side of the school building during lunch period. A crowd of students were milling about before the bell rang for the fifth period classes to begin. Guns were fired from both the front and the back seats of the car, spraying bullets among the students and teachers on lunch duty. The car then sped away before the stunned witnesses could react. One student, a 15-year-old girl, lay dead and three others were critically wounded. One of the injured later died in the hospital.

Police cars and helicopters blanketed the area searching for the culprits and assisting emergency vehicles. Word quickly spread throughout the neighborhood. Worried parents rushed to the school. Frightened students either left school or gathered together to express their outrage, disbelief, and grief.

Questions:

- What security measures need to be taken immediately?

- What could be done by the crisis team to contain the chaos?

- What steps would help control rumors?

- What guidelines for responding to the media would be followed?

- Should a community meeting be called? How soon should it be held? What should be included on the agenda? Who would be the facilitator?

- What follow-up services might be needed for students and teachers to help them recover from the emotional aftereffects of the crisis?

_____

Name of School

_____

Name of Principal

School Crisis Management Plan

_____

School Year

School Crisis Management Plan

Developing a School Crisis Plan

Pre-decisions are invaluable for those required to respond quickly and effectively when a crisis occurs. It may be difficult to give thorough and careful consideration to crisis procedures during an emergency. Many general procedures and decisions can be made ahead of time to guide administrators who have management responsibilities. Every school is encouraged to assign the task of developing a plan to the crisis team or another safety committee. The plan will be more effective if there are several people involved who will have a diversity of concerns and ideas. The crisis plan will then need to be reviewed by the whole faculty so the school community is familiar with the procedures and takes ownership in them.

The suggested strategies in this section can be adapted to fit the available resources and personnel. These strategies become the "standard operating procedures" for the school.

Situations will vary from facility to facility. No one campus plan can be made to apply to each facility. Plans should be put in writing, practiced, and reviewed annually to be kept up to date.

Answers to the following questions need to be included in any comprehensive campus plan. A format for such a plan follows this section.

- Who are the crisis team members? (Include backup members for the leaders.)

- What are their assigned responsibilities? What training will take place for the team members to understand their roles?

- How and when will the full staff receive orientation to the crisis plan?

- What rooms will be used for crisis counseling?

- Where will crisis coordination and the command post (with communication capability) be located?

- What area will be assigned to the media and who will be the media spokesperson?

- In the event of evacuation, what procedures will be followed? Have teachers been instructed to take their class attendance book with them? What system will be followed in reuniting children with their parents?

- How will information be disseminated to parents, students, staff, and administration?

- Who has a copy of the building's floor plan displaying room numbers, doors and windows, offices, and restrooms? Where is it kept?

- Have badges been made for all school staff involved in handling emergencies?

- Is there an adequate communication plan linking the classrooms, school yard, and all buildings with the office? Is there a coded warning system?

- What provisions have been made to address the special needs of handicapped students or those with limited English proficiency during a crisis?

- Are community leaders identified who can assist in creating and maintaining a safe school environment?

- Are community resources identified that are available to assist in reducing traumatic effects following major crises?

- What preventive safety measures are in place or planned?

Targets and Strategies*

Target 1: To Establish a Campus Crisis Team

■ Who are the team members and what are their assigned roles and responsibilities? Be flexible in determining which functions best fit the needs of your school and your personnel resources.

Name	Responsibilities

1. _____

2. _____

3. _____

4. _____

5. _____

6. _____

7. _____

*Note: Targets and Strategies has been adapted from the Dallas Schools' *Emergency Handbook* and *Emergency Manual.*

■ Who are the backup people for key team members in case of absence?

_____

_____

_____

_____

_____

Target 2: To Have a Prepared Plan for Sharing Information during a Crisis*

■ District personnel to contact

Name _____ Phone _____

Name _____ Phone _____

Name _____ Phone _____

Name _____ Phone _____

Name _____ Phone _____

Name _____ Phone _____

Name _____ Phone _____

■ How will the staff be informed and the plan activated if the event has taken place before or after school hours?

_____

_____

_____

_____

*A telephone tree form can be found on page 58.

21

■ What warning system will be used if there is an emergency during school hours?

_____

_____

_____

_____

■ What mechanism is there for disseminating information during schools hours? How will this vary with different types of crises?

_____

_____

_____

_____

■ What is the communication linkage between the outlying or portable buildings and security personnel?

_____

_____

_____

_____

■ What are the plans to keep the parents and community informed?

_____

_____

_____

_____

■ Other

_____

_____

_____

_____

Target 3: To Prepare School Personnel to Respond Effectively to Crises

■ What is the strategy to train the safety and crisis team? Include dates, trainers, arrangements and agenda.

_____

_____

_____

_____

■ How will the full staff receive orientation to the safety and crisis plan?

_____

_____

_____

_____

Target 4: To Use the Building in an Efficient Manner in the Event of a Crisis

■ What provisions have been made to orient emergency workers to the building's layout?

_____

■ Where are the up-to-date floor plan and room assignments kept?

_____

_____

_____

_____

■ List all hazardous material/chemicals and storage location on campus (e.g., cleaning fluids, chemistry lab, art classroom storage, etc.)

_____

_____

_____

_____

■ Which rooms will be designated for individual and/or group counseling?

_____

_____

_____

_____

■ Where will a command post/crisis coordination headquarters be located?

_____

_____

_____

■ What room will be utilized for media activities?

_____

_____

_____

_____

■ Other

_____

_____

_____

_____

Target 5: To Make Provisions for Special Populations

■ What special needs would handicapped or students with limited English proficiency have during a crisis?

_____

_____

_____

■ What provisions have been made to meet these needs?

_____

_____

_____

_____

Target 6: To Use Community Resources to Prevent and Resolve Crises in Schools

■ Identify community leaders who can assist schools in creating and maintaining a physically safe and emotionally positive school environment.

_____

_____

_____

_____

■ Identify available community resources to assist in reducing the traumatic effects of loss and devastation following major crises.

_____

_____

_____

_____

Target 7: To Maintain a Safe Environment for Students and Staff

■ Needs Assessment (incidents from the previous year)

1. How many students were identified as having violated the drug policy?

_____

Give a breakdown of actions taken:

_____

_____

_____

_____

2. What evidence of gang activity was identified in or near the school?

- ❑ Graffiti
- ❑ Students wearing colors, jewelry, clothing
- ❑ Retaliation or initiation-motivatedfights
- ❑ Drive-by shootings

- ❑ Increase in truancy rate
- ❑ Increase in number of racial incidents
- ❑ Use of beepers, pagers, and cellular phones

3. How many weapons were found on campus? _____

Give a breakdown of actions taken.

_____

_____

_____

_____

4. List the assaults and physical altercations which occurred on campus. What injuries to students occurred? Were there any injuries to staff?

_____

_____

_____

_____

5. List incidents of vandalism or theft.

_____

_____

_____

_____

6. List other incidents requiring discipline management and actions taken.

_____

_____

_____

_____

7. Compare truancy, suspensions, home-study, and expulsion rates to previous years.

_____

_____

_____

8. How many suicide threats, attempts, and completions occurred on campus? _____

   How many were reported to have occurred off campus? _____

9. How many other homicides, natural or accidental deaths of students or staff were there? _____

10. How many child abuse cases were reported? _____

11. Outline any accidental injuries that took place regarding students or staff.

_____

_____

_____

_____

■ Prevention Measures

1. Identify physical barriers and suggestions for altering the facility that would improve safety (i.e., lighting, fences, locks, etc.).

_____

_____

_____

_____

2. What other safety measures are in place or planned, such as limiting access to the building, an identification system, electronic locks, closed-circuit TV, or improving communication between schoolyard and portable buildings?

_____

_____

_____

_____

3. What arrangements are in place or planned for dispute mediation and conflict resolution training and utilization?

_____

_____

_____

_____

4. List safety topics addressed at faculty meetings or staff development.

_____

_____

_____

What safety training has the faculty received for preventing assaults?

_____

_____

_____

_____

5. What efforts are being made or planned for addressing youth violence and gang activity?

_____

_____

_____

_____

6. What suicide prevention measures are in place or planned?

_____

_____

_____

_____

7. What educational efforts have been made or planned to assist faculty in recognizing abuse or other forms of victimization?

_____

_____

_____

_____

8. Is violence-reduction instruction included in the school's curricula?

❑ Yes   ❑ No

If yes, which curriculum is used? How many students receive or will receive this instruction?

_____

_____

_____

_____

9. What is the evacuation plan in case of emergency?

_____

_____

_____

_____

What system will be followed to reunite young children with parents?

_____

_____

_____

_____

10. What efforts have been made or planned to involve parents in cooperative efforts to reduce the potential for crisis?

_____

_____

_____

11. List any additional safety strategies.

_____

_____

_____

_____

School Safety Suggestions

A school climate conducive to an encouraging learning atmosphere begins with the feeling that school is a safe place to be. Planning for crisis management includes careful consideration of measures that address the prevention of crisis situations. Students, parents, staff, and faculty are vitally interested in their own security and often have creative and realistic ideas to improve safety features at school. The following suggestions are intended to stimulate additional ideas based on the school's needs and resources.

- Written student code of conduct

- Violence reduction curriculum (conflict resolution)

- Staff training for preventing assaults

- Teacher orientation regarding discipline plan and classroom management

- Student orientation regarding behavior expectations

- Peer dispute mediation training

- Suicide prevention curriculum

- Time-out area for cooling off

- Metal detectors

- Limited access to entryways; minimal entrances

- Front door monitoring

- Electronic locks on outside doors

- Visitor sign-in system

- Parking lot guards

- Fences and gates for parking lot

- Sufficient lighting throughout campus

- No access to secluded areas both inside and outside the building

- Walkie talkies

- Two-way communication to portables and all classrooms

- Coded alarm for emergency signal

- ID badges

- Removal of graffiti

- Reporting and enforcing all weapon and drug offenses, and other crimes

- Adhering to dress code

- Gang prevention activities

- Student and parent safety councils

- Familiarity with neighborhood police officers

- Video cameras

- Volunteer crossing guards

- Principals and teachers visible in lunchrooms, corridors, and halls

- School/neighborhood watch program

- Joint faculty/student restrooms

- Mixed faculty/student parking

- Parent center in school

- Creation of school pride and ownership campaign

- Strong extracurricular program

- Identification and supervision of known juvenile offenders

School Crisis Plan Review and Evaluation

School _____

Principal _____

Target	Not Included in the Plan	Partially Complete or Needs Improvement	Complete and Appropriate
Crisis Team			
1. Crisis team members and backup for leaders are identified.	❑	❑	❑
2. Responsibilities and roles are clear.	❑	❑	❑
Communication			
3. There are plans to disseminate information to parents, staff, and administration	❑	❑	❑
4. A communication system linking classrooms, schoolyard, and all buildings with the office is present. A coded warning system is chosen.	❑	❑	❑
Training and Orientation			
5. Training has taken place or is planned.	❑	❑	❑
6. All staff has or will receive orientation.	❑	❑	❑
Use of Building			
7. Crisis counseling rooms are designated.	❑	❑	❑
8. Location for crisis coordination/command post (with telephone) is identified.	❑	❑	❑
9. An area is assigned to the media and a media spokesperson is chosen.	❑	❑	❑
Special Populations			
10. Provisions have been made to address the special needs of handicapped or limited English proficiency students.	❑	❑	❑

Target	Not Included in the Plan	Partially Complete or Needs Improvement	Complete and Appropriate
11. A copy of building's floor plan showing room numbers, doors, windows, offices, and restrooms is available.	❑	❑	❑
12. Evacuation procedures and a system for reuniting children with parents are evident.	❑	❑	❑
13. Adequate preventative safety measures are in place or planned.	❑	❑	❑
14. Community leaders who will assist in creating and maintaining a safe school environment are identified.	❑	❑	❑
15. Available community resources to assist in the reduction of traumatic effects following a major crisis are identified.	❑	❑	❑

Particular Strengths and Creative Areas of the Plan

_____

_____

_____

Areas for Improvement

_____

_____

_____

Additional Comments

_____

_____

_____

_____

Reviewer _____

Date _____

37

Crisis Drills

The purpose of a crisis drill is to assist the school in its preparation and training for an actual crisis situation. The drill reveals the adequacy of the written crisis plan and how familiar the crisis team members are with their roles. It should be considered a learning experience. Observers should be familiar with the school's crisis plan and use their evaluations to point out the strengths and well as which sections or assigned responsibilities need revision. Hospitals, airports, and city emergency preparedness offices are required by law to conduct such exercises at least annually to keep them in a state of readiness.

An Emergency Management Exercise

The most effective drill would include strategies to make it as realistic as possible. One way to do this is to have people actually role play the major parts of the crisis in a full-scale exercise. The anxiety and tension may be realistic even though it is only a simulated crisis.

For example, in a suicide scenario, players could be assigned ahead of time to be the victim, the teacher, a witness, a frightened parent, and a reporter. Each player could wear a sign identifying which role he or she is playing. A briefing session with some instructions prior to the exercise would be helpful for the role players and observers or evaluators. Emergency services and outside resources should not be called or brought into the role play unless they have been part of the planning and prior arrangements have been made for them to participate.

A crisis drill can be conducted as a table-top exercise instead of a full-scale exercise. Role players acting out the parts of the crisis would not be involved in this type of a drill. Using a narrative such as Sample Crisis Drill Scenarios on pages 44–46, the crisis team would gather around a conference table and report their various roles as if the particular case were to really occur.

In either type of drill the school should not be told ahead of time the scenario to be used. The observation team and role players may simply appear at a prearranged time. The drills should be carried out with a minimum of disruption to classes and students.

The school's neighbors as well as parents and students need to be told that a drill is scheduled for a given time on a given day to avoid any panic or confusion. Younger children still may have difficulty separating make-believe from reality so it is advisable to conduct the drill away from areas that are visible to them. A full-scale kidnapping drill was once conducted in a second-grade classroom and, even though the children and their parents had been told the day before it was only an exercise, several of the youngsters had nightmares that night.

The observation checklist may be completed by the observation team or evaluators as the drill is practiced. Feedback should be given to the crisis team immediately following the drill in a debriefing session.

Criteria for evaluation of a crisis drill relates to the written plan. The following is an example of items that may be included.

Observation Checklist

		Yes	No	Does Not Apply
1.	The crisis team demonstrated familiarity with their plan.	❑	❑	❑

Comments:

_____

_____

| 2. | The team responded in a timely fashion. | ❑ | ❑ | ❑ |

Comments:

_____

_____

| 3. | A clear chain of command was observed. | ❑ | ❑ | ❑ |

Comments:

_____

_____

| 4. | First aid for injured students/staff were given priority. | ❑ | ❑ | ❑ |

Comments:

_____

_____

| 5. | Plans were clearly stated to contact emergency services. | ❑ | ❑ | ❑ |

Comments:

_____

_____

		Yes	No	Does Not Apply
6.	A plan of action for restoring order and directing students was evident.	❑	❑	❑

Comments:

_____

_____

| 7. | The appropriate district personnel were notified. | ❑ | ❑ | ❑ |

Comments:

_____

_____

| 8. | Procedures for contacting parents of victims or injured students were clear. | ❑ | ❑ | ❑ |

Comments:

_____

_____

| 9. | Provisions were made to inform faculty and student body. | ❑ | ❑ | ❑ |

Comments:

_____

_____

| 10. | Preparations were made to counsel students and staff individually or in groups. | ❑ | ❑ | ❑ |

Comments:

_____

_____

	Yes	No	Does Not Apply
11. Plans were made to debrief after school was dismissed.	❑	❑	❑

Comments:

_____

_____

	Yes	No	Does Not Apply
12. Evidence was shown that the media were handled appropriately by a designated spokesperson.	❑	❑	❑

Comments:

_____

_____

	Yes	No	Does Not Apply
13. Emphasis on teamwork was exhibited.	❑	❑	❑

Comments:

_____

_____

	Yes	No	Does Not Apply
14. A fact sheet was prepared for the secretary to respond to inquiries.	❑	❑	❑

Comments:

_____

_____

	Yes	No	Does Not Apply
15. Plans were made to use a coded emergency alert system.	❑	❑	❑

Comments:

_____

_____

		Yes	No	Does Not Apply

16. The building floor plan was available.   ❏   ❏   ❏

Comments:

_____

_____

17. Evidence was shown that the staff knew evacuation procedures.   ❏   ❏   ❏

Comments:

_____

_____

18. Parent and community concerns were considered.   ❏   ❏   ❏

Comments:

_____

_____

19. Needs of handicapped or special populations were accounted for.   ❏   ❏   ❏

Comments:

_____

_____

Sample Crisis Drill Scenarios

Exercise 1: An Angry Student with a Gun in Secondary School

An angry student with a gun in his backpack book bag enters the school at mid-morning. He has been suspended for three days for fighting and was told to bring his father for an appointment with the principal. When he reaches the main office he shouts that he has a gun and will make everyone in this school sorry, especially the security officer and the assistant principal. He says that his dad is on his way and they will turn this place into a war zone.

At this point the student dashes out of the main office and enters the security office where he continues screaming and threatening to shoot whomever tries to mess with him. He has his hand in the book bag waving it wildly at people, the windows, the hallway, etc. The gun discharges and wounds the student in his own leg. (Do not use either a real or toy gun in the drill.)

While the student is still in the security office a reporter who has picked up the emergency call from the police dispatcher on his radio enters the school building carrying a camera.

A parent who lives near the school hears the commotion and sees emergency vehicles pull up to the school. She runs into the building wanting to protect her daughter who is in a classroom on the second floor.

Exercise 2: The Arrest of an Elementary School Teacher

The evening news reports the arrest of a 33-year-old male for the possession and sale of child pornography. He has a previous arrest for child molestation in another state and was given a probated sentence. A search of his apartment turns up hundreds of sexually explicit photographs of children. The person arrested is

44

identified as a fourth-grade teacher who has taught in the district for five years.

The next morning the principal is contacted by detectives. Outraged parents call both the school and central administration threatening a lawsuit and demanding the dismissal of the teacher, principal, and superintendent. All of the television networks park their vans in front of the school and begin live coverage of the students as they arrive for classes and a group of very angry parents.

Exercise 3: The Death of an Elementary School Teacher

A teacher has collapsed in the school cafeteria during lunch period. She stops breathing and appears to have died. The principal is out of the building attending a meeting. One teacher sends a student to the nurse, and another begins CPR. Some of the children become hysterical and run out of the cafeteria, others begin crying and beg to go home. The deceased teacher's own child attends the second grade at the school. She also has an older child in a middle school. She has taught in the district for seven years and was named teacher of the year two years ago.

Exercise 4: The Suicide of a Secondary School Student

A 16-year-old junior walks to the front of a drama class during second period. Without saying anything, he puts a gun in his mouth and pulls the trigger. At first the stunned classmates think the scene was staged but soon realize the horror of his dead body. One student runs to the principal's office shouting what has happened. Pandemonium erupts among the students as word quickly spreads throughout the building. Some students who witnessed the suicide become hysterical and the teacher is visibly shaken. The suicide victim recently transferred to this school from another high school following his parents' divorce. He has siblings in elementary and middle schools. The media picks up the emergency call to the police and several reporters arrive at the school within minutes.

Students begin leaving school and the phone lines become tied up with calls from anxious parents.

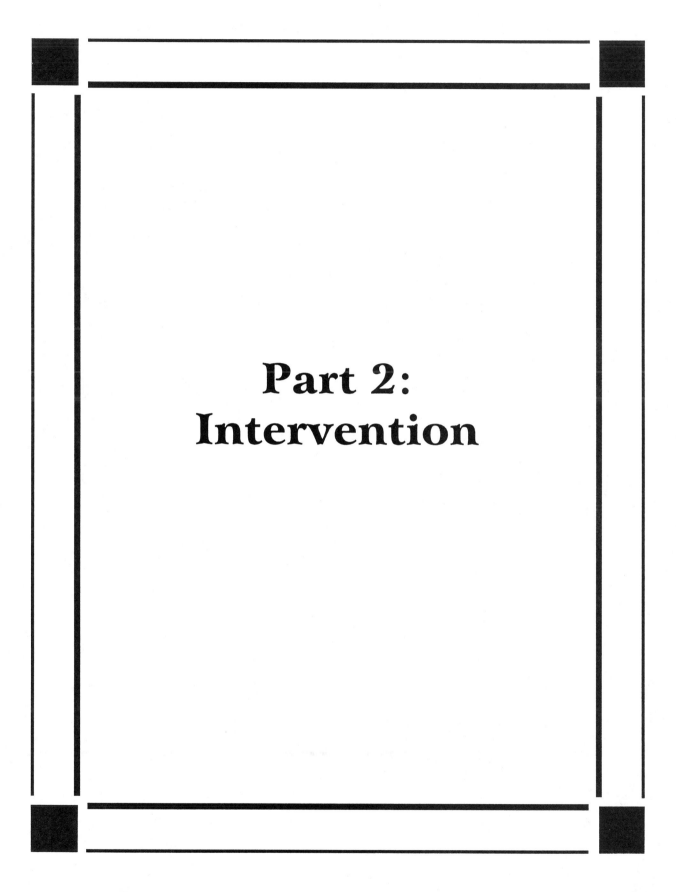

Part 2:
Intervention

An Introduction
to Intervention

Despite all the preventative and preparation measures taken by school administrators, a crisis is likely to happen at some time. A serious incident may not be an annual occurrence but, when it does happen, a school with a viable crisis plan in place that follows suggested crisis management steps will be able to contain the chaos and return the school to its normal functioning level sooner.

A crisis is easier to manage if the tragedy or traumatic event occurs after school hours. The principal and crisis team will have time to come to grips with any personal loss and be able to decide which segments of the crisis plan need to be put into place first. A telephone tree can notify teachers of a faculty meeting before school and give them time to also deal with any loss before facing the students.

Sometimes advanced warning is not possible. For example, a popular high school senior decided to have lunch with a friend off campus. Leaving the campus without parent permission was against the school policy. When the friend came into the school building to pick her up, a school secretary observed his behavior and was concerned that he might be intoxicated. A school security officer turned him away but, in spite of the officer's efforts, the girl left the building with him. Within minutes the young couple was in a serious automobile accident and the girl was killed. Word about the accident quickly spread throughout the school. Disbelief, anger, and grief disrupted most classes. The school secretary and security officer were distraught. The principal quickly called the crisis team to action and instructed teachers to set aside their instructional plans for the afternoon.

Since this incident happened while school was in session, there was little opportunity for the principal to spend time consulting or seeking advice. The crisis team needed to act quickly to minister to the grieving students and teachers.

The most severe crises affecting schools result from a death or serious injury to a student or teacher. The emotional impact of the shock and grief will interrupt any curriculum plans. Scheduled events or examinations will have to be postponed as crisis counselors and psychologists help students accept the reality of what has happened and sort out their feelings.

Other types of crises happen when the potential for danger arises and quick action is necessary to protect the students. One elementary school experienced this when noxious fumes from an unknown source was spread by the ventilation system throughout one wing of the building. Not recognizing the danger immediately, the principal moved the children to the auditorium and then to the cafeteria further away from the smelly classrooms. Soon some teachers and students developed breathing difficulties and became nauseated. A full-scale evacuation was ordered and emergency crews were called to the building. Ambulances transported those most affected to a hospital and paramedics attempted to examine all other children while anxious parents, seeing the police cars, fire trucks, and helicopters hovering above, rushed to the school to find their children. The staff was faced with all the elements of a serious crisis while supervising over 800 students at a nearby evacuation center. An incident command center system would be an asset during the management of a crisis of this magnitude. The incident command center system outlined in this section is similar to those used by police and fire departments.

Communication

Communication is the key to effective crisis management. All crisis plans need systems to inform those in a position to assist with the crisis management or to inform those affected by the event who have to deal with the emotional impact. The crisis might escalate if they do not know the true facts. A portion of this section includes an outline of a fact sheet and sample memos and letters that may be adapted to inform the parents and faculty.

The Media

The media usually plays a significant role during a major school crisis. The public is always interested in the happenings at a school and the disruption that occurs during a crisis is usually newsworthy. Reporters will get their story and it is best they get it from a school spokesperson. Refusing to give an interview only means the information will come from a source that may not be as reliable. The media guidelines in this section are similar to those adapted by the American Association of Suicidology and have proven to be useful by many school administrators.

Twenty-nine Crisis Situations

It is difficult for a school administrator to think of everything that needs attention during the heat of an actual crisis. The steps for crisis management in this intervention section of the manual address 29 different situations that might require crisis management strategies. The situations are identified according to the level of impact they are likely to have on the school. They are organized for quick reference and are intended to be used as suggested guidelines. Please note that any particular situation may introduce an aspect that will have to be dealt with but may not be included in these guidelines because each crisis and each school is unique. The 29 that are listed in this manual take into consideration most aspects of a crisis but flexibility is always recommended in order to adjust to the uniqueness of the situation.

Communication Suggestions for Crisis Management

Accurate and timely communication is the key to effective crisis management. The flow of information aids in decision making, brings necessary assistance, stifles the spread of rumors, reassures concerned parents, and helps begin the healing process for those emotionally devastated by a tragedy. The school principal assumes the lead in the management of crises occurring on or affecting a school campus and has the responsibility for the implementation of the school crisis plan. The principal gives instruction to call the security or emergency services, confers with the district administration, initiates crisis team activities, communicates with the faculty and students, and informs parents, and the public through letters, community meetings, or media interviews.

Communication and Crisis Management

There may be an erroneous tendency on the part of some administrators to order the staff not to discuss certain upsetting events with the false hope of keeping everything quiet enough to prevent students from getting upset and reacting emotionally. Unfortunately this cloak of secrecy only seems to add fuel to the fire. For example, if a student dies by suicide, talking about it will not cause more suicides but is more likely to help students begin the grief process. People tend to fill in any lack of information with rumors and stories that escalate the seriousness of the situation. The truth is easier to accept than anxiety-producing fear of the unknown. Dealing openly with this taboo subject teaches young people how to recognize suicide warning signs and respond appropriately to a friend who may be contemplating suicide. Crisis counseling may actually prevent another suicide. Correct postvention efforts become effective suicide prevention.

Communication Flow Chart

A diagram may clarify the communication process. The principal is at the top of the flow chart. Most crisis management steps begin with verification of information. Once the principal has done this he or she may follow this chart as a reminder who need to be contacted. Each arrow may not need to be followed for a Level 1 crisis. The whole chart might need to be filled for a major Level 3 crisis.

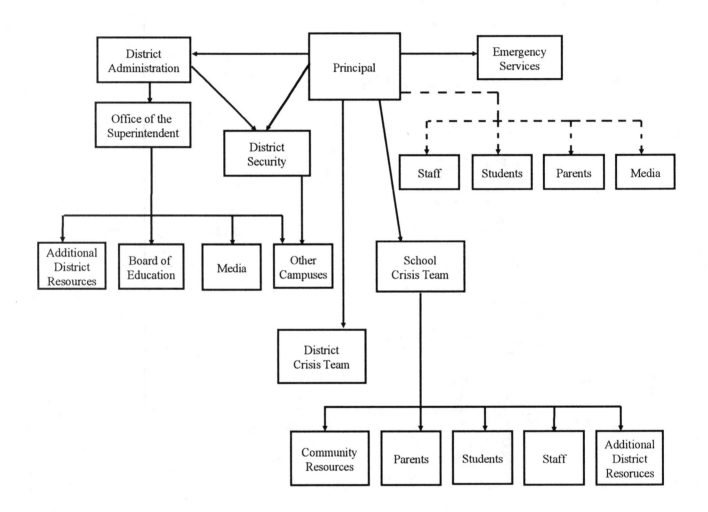

Emergency Telephone Numbers

City Emergency Services: Fire, Police, Paramedics   911

School District Resources

District Security   _____

Health Services   _____

Psychological/Social/Counseling Services   _____

District Administration   _____

Employee Relations/Personnel   _____

Communications/Public Relations   _____

Other   _____

Community Resources

Child Welfare/Child Protective Services   _____

Crisis Center   _____

Mental Health Services   _____

Poison Control   _____

Rape Crisis Center   _____

Runaway Hotline   _____

Other   _____

Telephone Tree
for Contacting Faculty

Depending on the size of the faculty and staff, extend a chart similar to this. Each person on the list calls the next person. If that person is not home, leave a message, skip, and call the following on the list.

Name _____

| Name _____ | Name _____ | Name_____ |
| Phone _____ | Phone _____ | Phone_____ |

| Name _____ | Name _____ | Name_____ |
| Phone _____ | Phone _____ | Phone_____ |

| Name _____ | Name _____ | Name_____ |
| Phone _____ | Phone _____ | Phone_____ |

| Name _____ | Name _____ | Name_____ |
| Phone _____ | Phone _____ | Phone_____ |

| Name _____ | Name _____ | Name_____ |
| Phone _____ | Phone _____ | Phone_____ |

| Name _____ | Name _____ | Name_____ |
| Phone _____ | Phone _____ | Phone_____ |

| Name _____ | Name _____ | Name_____ |
| Phone _____ | Phone _____ | Phone_____ |

| Name _____ | Name _____ | Name_____ |
| Phone _____ | Phone _____ | Phone_____ |

| Name _____ | Name _____ | Name_____ |
| Phone _____ | Phone _____ | Phone_____ |

| Name _____ | Name _____ | Name_____ |
| Phone _____ | Phone _____ | Phone_____ |

| Name _____ | Name _____ | Name_____ |
| Phone _____ | Phone _____ | Phone_____ |

| Name _____ | Name _____ | Name_____ |
| Phone _____ | Phone _____ | Phone_____ |

Sample Fact Sheet

To answer telephone inquires during a crisis, know the facts:

1. What has happened?

    _____

    _____

    _____

    _____

2. When did the event occur?   _____

3. Where did the event occur?   _____

4. Who is involved? (Do not give out names of deceased or injured until the family has been notified.)

    _____

    _____

    _____

5. What is being done by school and emergency personnel?

    _____

    _____

    _____

6. What procedure should parents follow to have their children/students released or excused to attend a funeral?

_____

_____

_____

7. Will the school be closed or classes held in another facility? If so, where?

_____

8. Are any meetings planned for parents or members of the community? When? Where?

_____

_____

_____

9. What is being planned to help families directly affected by the crisis?

_____

_____

_____

Sample Faculty Memo

Date:

To: Westview faculty and staff

From: James Decker, Principal

Subject: Suicide of John Smith

We are asking you to discuss the death of John Smith, an eighth grade Westview student, with your class at the beginning of school. Smith students will already be aware of his suicide from the 10:00 p.m. news on TV last night. Others will be learning of his death from you. I recommend that you give your class an opportunity to hear the following facts from you first, then give them time to ask questions and discuss their feelings. You can expect some students to be angry and upset as well as sad. Please be sensitive to their feelings.

John died last night at 8:00 p.m. after hanging himself in his closet with a rope. He was discovered by his father and rushed by ambulance and paramedics to the emergency room of the county hospital where the trauma doctors and nurses were unable to revive him. He did not regain consciousness and died one-half hour after he arrived. The medical examiner has ruled his death a suicide. His parents would like you to know that they have donated some of his body organs so other may have a chance to live. We do not know why John chose to kill himself. Unfortunately, he did not realize what other options were available to help him with his problems. His solution was permanent and irreversible.

Students may be excused from classes for John's funeral if they bring a written excuse from a parent. Funeral arrangements are still pending. We will give you that information when we receive it. The family will be at the funeral home tomorrow evening if anyone wishes to pay his or her respects and extend sympathy. Some students may wish to make a donation to the Crisis Center in John's memory. A box is placed in the office for the collection of donations or any notes written to John's family.

The crisis team will be in the school building throughout today and the rest of the week. If you wish some assistance in discussing John's death with your class, a team member will come to your classroom. Please identify any student you think needs further help in dealing with this tragic event and send him or her to the counselor's office.

Today may be a very difficult one for you as well as our students. A crisis team member will be in the teachers' lounge if you wish to talk futher about the suicide.

Sample Faculty Memo

Date:

To: Southlake Elementary faculty and staff

From: Wendell Connor, Principal

Subject: Accident on campus

We have had a serious injury of a student in one of the third-grade classrooms early this afternoon. You may have heard the commotion and seen emergency personnel enter the building. Your students may be anxious and upset. Please only tell them there has been an accident and the police and firemen are here to help. Encourage them to express their fears and scary feelings. The sirens and ambulance may remind them of other accidents in their neighborhood or home. Reassure them that there is no danger to them.

Do not permit students to enter the south hallway at this time. Exit the building and re-enter through the west entrance to reach the cafeteria or gym. If your classroom is located in the south wing, remain in class until you receive further notice.

We will identify the student for you after the family has been contacted and will give you additional information as soon as it is available. There will be a faculty meeting in the media center at 3:35 p.m. with the crisis team and the school psychologist. Please plan to attend.

Sample Letter to Parents

Date:

Dear Parents of Westview Students:

The Westview Middle School community was saddened to learn of the reported suicide of one of our students. The death of any young person is a loss which, in one way or another, affects each of us. The tragic circumstances of John Smith's death are perhaps more shocking and more difficult to accept.

We have asked the assistance of the crisis team to help our school community deal with this loss. We are doing everything we can to help your child and our staff through this tragic experience. You may anticipate more questions and a need to talk bout the suicide at home.

John's funeral will be held at Grace Baptist Church, 428 Elm Street, on Thursday at 10:30 a.m. Your child may be excused from school to attend the funeral with written permission from you. We encourage you to make arrangements to accompany him or her. You will need to provide your own transportation. The school will remain open for those students who choose not to attend the funeral.

John's classmates and teachers have decided to receive donations in his memory and will make a contribution to the Crisis Center. Please contact the school office at 823-1000 for further information.

If you have any concerns regarding your child's reactions to this loss, Mrs. Jones, the school nurse, and Mr. Johnston, the school counselor, will be available to assist you.

Sincerely,

James Decker, Principal
Westview Middle School

Sample Letter to Parents

Date:

Dear Parents:

The school is deeply saddened by the death of Mrs. Harriett Morrison, one of our fourth grade teachers. Mrs. Morrison had been a member of our faculty for seven years. We will miss her. She was found in her home over the weekend and the police suspect the cause of death was homicide. We have no additional information to give you about the shocking event of her death at this time.

Your child's class had the opportunity to talk to a school psychologist from the crisis team today about our loss. You may expect your child to want to talk to you about his or her feelings when they get home from school. As difficult as it is, talking about feelings will help them deal with the death.

The funeral will be on Tuesday, September 19 at 11:00 a.m. at the St. Rita's Episcopal Church, 6720 Webster. Smith and Johnson Funeral Home, 1802 North Washington, is in charge of the service. We encourage you to accompany and support your child if you want him or her to attend the service. The school office needs a written note from you in order for us to release your child from class.

Please telephone the school counselor or school psychologist if you would like further help or assistance.

Sincerely,

Mrs. Marilyn Brown
Principal

Media Guidelines

Suggested Guidelines for Responding to the Media

The following list of suggestions for working with the media will assist in minimizing the disruption during a school crisis and in informing the public about a newsworthy event.

1. Direct all media inquiries to the principal or designated spokesperson. This avoids confusion in times of a crisis and ensures consistency of information given to the media. When the spokesperson is unavailable, the school secretary or another designated person should have a fact sheet containing pertinent information from which to answer telephone inquires.

2. Do not permit interviews with students or staff on the premises during a crisis and do not permit filming inside the building except in the spokesperson's office or designated media room.

3. Set up a comfortable room close to the entrance of the building that may be used by the media in the event of a Level 3 crisis. The room should have a telephone for use by media representatives. Offering coffee and soft drinks is a hospitable gesture. The media may prefer to remain outside the building with their crew and ask for individual interviews with the principal. A press conference is preferable because of the demands on the principal at the time of the crisis but individual interviews over the phone or in person is an acceptable alternative.

4. The spokesperson needs to respond to the media in a timely and professional manner. Avoid being defensive. Do not treat the interviewer as an adversary. Acknowledge the difficulty of the media's role and take a position of helpfulness.

5. The spokesperson should prepare a written statement or notes with points to be made for quick reference. If the answer to a question is not known, a return call with the information may be made. Release factual information only. Do not make assumptions.

6. Do not disclose personal information about any staff member or student. Personal information should be released only at the discretion of the family.

7. Drop the jargon or "educational vocabulary" in communicating with the media during a time of crisis. Say what you mean in simple terms.

8. Emphasize what is being done by the school and the district to contain and resolve the crisis.

9. If the school district has a communications department, one of their representatives may be asked to organize press conferences or set up individual interviews for the principal. Or the representative may be asked to personally give information to the media.

The Incident Command Center

When the safety of students and staff is threatened and on the occasion when a school building is evacuated the command center becomes the location for receiving and dispatching critical information and instruction to emergency services, campus and district administrators, and the crisis team. There may be a chemical spill, severe weather, fire, bombing, or potential violence. Fire departments and police departments usually operate under a similar system.

Purpose

When the city's emergency services are called to a school, the incident command center system should help with communication between the school and the emergency personnel. The purpose is to bring the situation under control as expediently as possible. Decisions will be made and directions given at this command center.

Activation

The principal, or designee in his or her absence, will activate the center when a major crisis affects the campus and requires extensive coordination.

Suggested Procedures

The nature of the crisis would dictate the specific activities of the incident command center. General operating procedures might include:

1. The principal is in charge of the site and is responsible for making decisions with the advice and consultation from the district administration.

2. When the city's emergency services are involved, the principal will follow instructions from the police bureau chief or the fire battalion chief who is in charge of their own field command post.

3. The actual location of the command center should be identified with a sign or other means for the emergency personnel arriving at the site to assist bringing the situation under control.

4. Additional communication capability should be a major consideration.

5. A liaison should be appointed to communicate with the fire or police field command post. The liaison will convey decisions and request information. This frees the principal to be more efficient in giving directions to the campus and district security staff or relaying information and requesting assistance from the district administration. Or the principal may assume this liaison position and appoint an assistant to be in charge of the staff and students. Whoever works with the field commander must have decision-making authority.

6. The location for releasing information to parents should be separate from the incident command center and also needs to be readily identifiable. Consideration may need to be given for bilingual capability, depending on the bilingual needs of the community.

7. No elementary age student should be released to an adult without proper identification. Account for each and every student.

Every teacher should take a class rollbook listing students' names to be used as a check-off when leaving the building for an evacuation.

8. If there are injuries, a crisis team member should be dispatched to the hospital. A list of all injured people and the location where they have been transported should be kept by these staff members who are meeting and giving information to parents. The crisis team members sent to the hospital will help keep the school informed about the condition of the injured.

9. If students are transported to another shelter site, such as a recreation center or another school, city buses or school buses may be used depending on prior arrangements. The principal may remain at the incident command center and appoint another administrator to be responsible for students at the shelter site or may choose to go with the students and appoint another administrator to be in charge of the incident command center.

10. The administrator sent to the relocation site should not allow children off the buses until specific arrangements have been agreed on with the shelter building's supervisor. A school staff person should be appointed to remain at the front desk area to answer questions.

11. The principal or principal's designee will be the school spokesperson for the media. A district spokesperson may be dispatched to the school to coordinate media interviews and ensure that information being released by the school is consistent with what is being released by the fire or police department. No permissions should be given for students to be interviewed or photographed inside the building.

12. The principal is responsible for documenting the sequences of the day's events, decisions made at the incident command center, and a summary of the post-incident crisis team debriefing.

Suggested Steps for Crisis Management

General Crisis Procedure Checklist for School Administrators

☐ 1. Determine the facts surrounding the crisis event, the crisis level, and potential impact

☐ 2. Request emergency services

☐ 3. Alert district administration

☐ 4. Ask that:

    ☐ a. Other schools likely to be affected by the crisis are notified

    ☐ b. Arrangements are made for additional district resources when necessary

☐ 5. Assemble and brief the local school crisis team, request that team members carry out pre-planned responsibilities

☐ 6. Designate rooms and space for counseling, media, and crisis coordination

☐ 7. Determine what information will be shared and with whom

    ☐ a. Memos, meetings, personal contact with faculty

    ☐ b. Letters to parents

    ☐ c. Fact sheet for secretary

    ☐ d. Statement for media

☐ 8. Debrief at the end of each day with all crisis team members (possibly midday on the first day)

☐ 9. Schedule additional planning sessions

☐ 10. Plan for parent/community meetings

*Note Communication Suggestions for Crisis Management has been adapted from the *Dallas Schools' Emergency Handbook* and *Emergency Manual*.

Crisis Management Guidelines — Level 1

Assault of a Student on Campus (Level 1)

Assisting the Victim

1. Provide medical attention if there are injuries.

2. Notify school security.

3. Unless injuries require the immediate attention of a doctor or indicate transfer to a hospital, keep the victim in the school clinic.

4. Notify the victim's parents. Anticipate the parents to emotionally overreact.

5. Notify district administration.

6. Provide counseling for the victim and his or her family. Help the victim regain a sense of security. Do not blame the victim. Respect cultural differences where, traditionally, outside counseling may not be acceptable and such matters are not shared beyond the immediate family.

If the Assault is a Rape

1. Contact the police (911), school security, and the victim's parents. The police will probably transport the assaulted individual to a hospital where he or she will be examined by specially trained personnel.

2. Ensure that a school nurse, counselor, psychologist, social worker, or a trusted friend remains with the victim until the police arrive.

3. Report information only to those directly involved with the victim's safety and well-being. Protect the identity of the victim. Notify district administration.

4. The school professional, who has been providing support, should remain with the victim and accompany the victim, police, and parents to the hospital.

5. Expect and prepare for questions from the media.

6. Reassure concerned parents regarding the safety precautions being taken at the school. A community or parent meeting may need to be scheduled if concern is widespread and cannot be resolved in individual exchanges.

7. Meet with parents and teachers of the victim to plan for his or her return to school.

8. Additional support or counseling may be desired or a school transfer may be considered to be in the best interest of the victim.

9. Log all activities and decisions.

10. Debrief with the crisis team.

Bomb Threat (Level 1)

1. Document the threat (time and date; exact words of caller; background noises; description of voice: sex, age if apparent, tone, and dialect).

2. Notify school security.

3. Inspect the building. Automatic dismissal or fire drill procedures are not standard practice for all bomb threats.

4. Notify the appropriate supervisor when a final check of the building has been completed.

Comments on Bomb Threat

All threats do not warrant calling the police. Unnecessary publicity, in fact, may encourage other incidents. Evaluate the threat. On the basis of evidence, experience, and judgment, decide whether the threat is credible.

Evidence

- Signs of illegal entry

- Report of missing chemicals

Experience

- Other threats have been hoaxes

- Tests are scheduled for that day

- Caller was obviously a youngster; giggling in background

- Unexplained student unrest

- Today is Senior Skip Day

Judgment

- Based on all available information, the threat is or is not credible

Bomb Found

1. Call police at 911.

2. Call school security.

3. Isolate the area.

4. If the fire alarm is to be used for evacuation, notify the fire department that the alarm was used because a bomb was located.

5. Evacuate the building in stages, starting with the rooms nearest the device. Instruct teachers to take their attendance sheets or role books with them.

6. Do not handle the device. Do not use a two-way radio. Do not attempt to dismantle or remove the device.

7. Notify district administration.

8. Re-enter the building only after being advised to do so by the police.

9. Prepare a statement for the media.

10. Provide a fact sheet to help the school secretary and others in answering the questions of concerned parents, including the location of evacuated students.

11. If concerned parents arrive at the school to remove their elementary school-age children, make arrangements to check identification. Release students only to a parent who has custody.

12. Document all decisions and actions taken.

Child Abuse or Neglect (Level 1)

1. Ensure that an oral report to child welfare or child protective services and/or the police department is made within 48 hours by the person who identifies or suspects abuse or neglect.

2. Do not attempt to verify the information.

3. Permit an interview with the child by authorized, properly identified officials only.

4. Do not notify parents. They will be notified by the investigators. The principal will be informed that this has been done before the child is released.

5. Ensure that the person who originally suspected the abuse or neglect files a written report within five days.

6. Provide follow-up counseling when appropriate.

7. Document all decisions and action taken.

Community or Political Protest Activity (Level 1)

1. Identify the group and the purpose of the protest.

2. Notify school security.

3. Notify police.

4. Notify district administration. Determine if mediation is needed.

5. If the group is disruptive, warn members they are in violation of the law and subject to arrest. Ask them to discontinue their activity.

6. Do not allow disruptive persons to enter school property. If the protest group is already on the school premises, request that the members vacate immediately. Assign staff to all building entrances to prevent further disturbances inside the facilities.

7. Advise teachers to keep classroom doors closed and locked, if possible.

8. Keep administrative offices locked; provide security measures for files and records.

9. Keep the faculty informed through memos, brief meetings, or through other campus communication systems.

10. Prepare a statement for the media.

11. Prepare for community meetings if needed to respond to the demands or problems identified by the protesters.

12. Refer to the school board policy for disciplinary action if students are involved in demonstrations and create or threaten to create a substantial disruption in classes or school- sponsored activities. Try to allow students the opportunity to voice opinions or dissent where they can be heard and appropriately responded to by administrators inside the building.

While most protest activities area appropriate to classify as a Level 1 crisis that can be managed with the resources at hand, there is a potential for them to escalate into a more serious situation and require additional action. If the situation escalates to threats or actual physical harm or damage to property, additional emergency procedures may be necessary. (See Level 3: Riot Developing from Community or Political Protest Activity.)

Contagious Disease (Level 1)

Rumor

1. Contact the health services district administrator for information.

2. Convene the local school crisis team.

3. Decide on and execute a plan — prepare a memo to be read in all classes, an announcement on the public address system, or a letter to parents — to disseminate information.

4. Meet with key students individually, or in groups, to show a unified stance on the issue. Use this situation to educate the students about the facts and the disease. If there is a rumor, educate the students about the meaning and dangers of rumors.

5. Prepare a fact sheet for the school secretary.

Actual

1. Contact the health services district administrator for information and instructions.

2. Convene the local school crisis team if the disease is serious and the principal and school nurse need assistance and support.

3. Prepare a fact sheet for the school secretary.

4. Using input from the health services administrator and the school nurse, decide on an approach that will best address the particular situation.

   - Students with a reportable disease may be excluded from attendance until:

     - a physician attests to their recovery,

     - the local health authority gives permission, or

- the appropriate time elapses and they are no longer contagious.

■ A meeting with concerned parents may be appropriate to dispel any rumors and provide accurate information regarding the incidence and implications of the disease.

■ Respect any cultural differences and a preference for privacy by some parents.

Cult Activity: Evidence of or Suspected (Level 1)

1. Verify information with help from personnel familiar with cults.

2. Consult with the school psychologist.

3. Photograph evidence of suspected cult activities (mutilated animal carcasses, jars of blood, candles, altars, graffiti, etc.)

4. Remove the evidence after contacting school security.

5. Attempt to identify the students involved.

6. Inform parents or guardians of students involved and express your concerns. Some cultures may view these activities as common in their native environments.

7. Follow standard disciplinary procedures for any offense committed, such as defacement of property.

8. Schedule a faculty meeting or workshop to educate school personnel about signs, symbols, and what to look for in students who may be involved in any cult activity.

9. Request assistance from additional specialists if drugs are involved or suicidal ideation is present. This crisis may escalate to Level 2 and require other additional outside assistance if the evidence is bizarre and witnessed by uninvolved students.

Dangerous or Irate Person on Campus (Level 1)

1. Alert school security.

2. Check identification if possible. Determine whether the person has a legitimate reason to be on campus. As a precaution, have backup for support.

3. If the person cannot give identification or legitimate reason for being on campus, notify police. Ask the person to leave or, if necessary, have the person removed.

4. The situation would become an emergency if:

    - the personal safety of the students, faculty, or staff is threatened,

    - the orderly management of the instructional program is disrupted, or

    - school order and discipline are disturbed.

5. If the person is identified as a parent or person with a legitimate reason to be there, utilize a combination of extreme politeness, courtesy, and firmness to structure and de-escalate the behavior. If the person is coherent, listen to him or her and try to understand the concerns. Do not permit a classroom to be disrupted.

6. If the situation was witnessed by students or staff, inform them of the facts once the situation is resolved.

7. Document all decisions and actions taken.

Death of Parent, Guardian, or
Significant Family Member (Level 1)

1. Contact the family to gather information about the circumstances of the death, funeral arrangements, and needs of the child and siblings. Although many families prefer to have their children at home during these times, others may prefer structure and social support and will send the child to school very soon after the death.

2. Share information with the student's classmates. Classmates may draw or write sympathy cards. Use the opportunity to discuss death, grief, and loss.

3. Visit the home. Note the religious and social customs of the family when timing the visit. It may be preferable to express sympathy at the wake instead of visiting the home.

4. Attend the funeral.

5. Prepare the classmates to be supportive when the student returns to school.

6. Provide counseling support when the student returns to school.

7. Monitor the student's academic performance throughout the year noting any difficulties, behavior problems, or depression that might be related to the family death.

Illness (Serious) of Student
or Faculty Member (Level 1)

1. Confirm the information from the ill person's family.

2. Inform the school staff after appropriate permission is granted.

3. Plan with the student's teacher or faculty substitute about sharing the information with classmates. Such planning might include writing letters or performing useful tasks for the ill person and his/her family.

4. Provide study materials for home or hospital-bound student.

5. Regularly update the faculty and classmates on the condition of the person who is ill.

6. Make plans for the return of the individual to school or for saying goodbye should withdrawal or resignation become necessary.

Suicide Attempt Off Campus (Level 1)

1. Meet with the student and his or her parents. Some cultures may regard a suicide attempt as a humiliation and prefer privacy.

2. Visit the student if he or she is hospitalized.

3. Identify friends of the student and provide counseling for them.

4. Formulate a re-entry plan with parents, the student, and appropriate staff to address the needs of the student when returning to school after an absence for hospitalization or treatment. If the student was treated at a hospital, a medical release should be required to return to school. If no medical assistance is needed, recommendations from the mental health professional who is seeing the student should be requested. Respect cultural differences or a desire for confidentiality by some parents.

Suicide Threat (High Risk) (Level 1)

1. Make sure that the student is not left alone, is under careful watch in a secure place, and does not have any means available to attempt suicide. Do not allow the student to leave campus alone. Release the student only to a parent or guardian. A trusted teacher or adult may remain with the student until the parent arrives.

2. Notify parents or guardians immediately.

3. Request assistance from the school psychologist.

4. If the student is to be seen for psychiatric emergency services and the parents are unavailable to transport, make sure the transporting individual has special insurance coverage. The school psychologist or counselor should accompany the suicidal student.

5. Determine if other students need to be involved in follow-up support services.

6. Formulate a re-entry plan with the student, parents, and appropriate staff to address the needs of the student on the return to school following an absence for hospitalization or treatment.

Violent Behavior of a Student (Level 1)

1. Notify school security if needed.

2. Remove the student from the class, using as little physical contact as required, with the assistance of available adults.

3. Place the student in a secure, secluded room for time out. Physically restrain if necessary.

4. Ask the nurse to assess the possibility of drug involvement.

5. Attempt to calm the student by listening and reassuring him or her.

6. Talk with the teacher and witnesses to find out exactly what happened.

7. Contact the parents. Describe the behavior of the student and the action taken by the school. Ask for their ideas about what might be wrong and for their help in planning to alleviate the difficulty.

8. Notify the school psychologist if the violent behavior has been intense, continuing, or if the student is handicapped.

9. Discuss the incident with other students who may have observed the violent behavior.

10. If the student is suspended, decide on steps needed for re-admitting the student.

11. Document all decisions and actions taken.

Weapons on Campus (Level 1)

Possession or Exhibition of a Firearm or Other Lethal Weapons

1. Confiscate the weapon.

2. Notify school security and the police department.

3. Hold an expulsion hearing with the parents, student, and appropriate school personnel present.

4. Expel the student if expulsion is required by school board policy.

5. Notify district administration and document all decisions and actions taken.

Gun Discharged

1. If a gun is discharged in the school building during school hours the crisis may escalate to a Level 2.

2. Call 911 for emergency assistance.

3. Request immediate assistance from school security to confiscate the weapon and apprehend the student.

4. If injuries are involved, follow Steps 2 through 16 under Accident with Severe Injuries (Level 2).

5. If there are no injuries:

   a. Remove all students from the area.

   b. Convene the local school crisis team.

   c. Inform teachers of the incident.

   d. Ask teachers to refer distressed students to a counselor or school psychologist.

Level 2

Abduction (Level 2)

Witnessed

1. Call 911 for immediate assistance.

2. Gather facts about the abduction and a description of the abductor from witnesses.

3. Notify parents of the child.

4. Notify district administration.

5. Convene the local school crisis team.

6. Decide on a plan of action, including:

   - Meet with faculty if possible. Advise teachers about sharing the information with students. Do not use the public address system for announcing initial information. Protect the abducted student's privacy concerning sexual molestation.

   - Visit classrooms if requested.

   - Prepare a statement for the media. Ask police about what information may be released.

   - Prepare a fact sheet to help those answering phone inquiries.

   - If concerned parents arrive at school to remove their elementary school-age children, make arrangement to check identification. Release children only to parents who have custody.

   - If concern exists about additional abductions, send letters home to elementary parents.

7. Prepare classmates to be supportive when the child is returned.

8. Provide for follow-up counseling as needed.

9. Document all decisions and activities.

10. Debrief with the crisis team.

Not Witnessed

1. Verify that the child is missing. Have the building searched.

2. Notify parents.

3. Notify school security.

4. Notify district administration.

5. Convene the local school crisis team.

6. Question the child's friends for information.

7. Ask school personnel to assist in searching the neighborhood, if prudent.

8. If the child is not found, call 911.

9. Follow steps #6 through #10 under Witnessed.

An Accident with Severe Injuries Involving Several Students (Level 2)

On Campus

1. Call 911 for emergency assistance.

2. Assess injuries.

3. Assist the nurse.

4. Remove uninjured students from the accident site.

5. Notify parents of the nature and extent of their children's injuries, and specify where their children are located.

6. Notify district administration.

7. Convene the local school crisis team.

8. Arrange for the counseling of witnesses and close friends of the injured.

9. Notify siblings of the injured on campus and counselors at other schools where siblings attend.

10. Inform teachers and all students of the accident. Do not use public address system. Send a memo or a member of the crisis team to the classrooms.

11. Ask teachers to refer distressed students to the counselor or crisis specialist.

12. Provide accurate information to those answering the questions of other parents or the community.

13. Prepare a statement for the media.

14. Visit injured students at the hospital.

15. Debrief with the crisis team.

16. Log all activities and decisions.

Off Campus

1. Verify information.

2. Notify the district administration.

3. Notify the local school crisis team.

4. Follow steps #8 through #15 under On Campus.

An Accusation Against School Personnel Related to Illegal Activities such as Child Abuse or Molestation (Level 2)

1. Document what has been reported. Do not investigate or attempt to verify the information.

2. Notify the employee relations or the personnel department and follow their instructions. The usual procedure is to place the accused on administrative leave with pay until the investigation is complete.

3. Notify district administration.

4. Report the accusation to the police department. If they choose not to investigate, report the incident to child welfare or child protective services.

5. Allow time for the employee to be interviewed and arrange for a substitute if necessary.

6. Convene the local school crisis team.

7. Provide for the police investigators if they come to the school. Notify the parents of the procedure.

8. Provide crisis counseling for children only after their statements have been taken by the police or child welfare workers.

9. Notify parents of affected students that initial crisis counseling is being provided. If additional counseling is needed, it will be provided with their permission. Always use "alleged" or "allegation" regarding the accusation.

10. Depending on the situation, in cooperation with the police and child welfare, prepare for:

    ■ A written statement to the media.

■ Inquires from irate, demanding, and scared parents. Prepare a fact sheet for the secretary.

■ A staff meeting to stop the spread of rumors and to update participants on the facts as known.

■ A parent meeting with district administrators to give reassurance that safety measures are begin taken to prevent future incidents and to allow questions and discussion.

11. Document all decisions and actions taken.

12. Debrief with the school crisis team.

Altercation or Violence between Groups or Gang Members (Level 2)

1. Request assistance from school security or police.

2. Re-establish order with assistance from available staff.

3. Assess the danger including injuries, number of students involved, location of altercation, and the presence or absence of weapons.

4. Provide first aid to injured students. Call paramedics (911) if injuries require further medical attention.

5. Notify district administration.

6. Convene the local school crisis team.

7. Interview witnesses and ask them to describe what led to the altercation.

8. Prepare plans to prevent retaliation or further campus violence.

   ■ Remove graffiti outside and inside school property, e.g. restroom walls.

   ■ Enforce dress code policy in order to reduce the easy identification of gang members.

   ■ Notify probation officers if any students involved are on probation.

   ■ Ask student leaders to recommend ways to resolve issues.

   ■ Facilitate discussion between gang or ethnic groups. Dispute mediation may be appropriate.

   ■ Conduct workshops for students and faculty focusing on ethnic or gang-related issues.

9. Ask the parents of involved students to come to school to discuss concerns leading to the violence. Follow disciplinary procedures to address any offense such as aggravated assault, possession of weapons, etc.

10. Prepare a statement for the media in conjunction with the police.

11. Prepare a fact sheet for telephone inquiries.

12. Reassure parents, students, and faculty that appropriate steps are being taken to ensure safety.

13. Document all decisions and actions taken.

14. Debrief with the school crisis team.

Death Off Campus: Natural, Accident, Homicide, or Suicide (Level 2)

1. Verify information.

2. Convene the local school crisis team.

3. Notify the district administration.

4. Meet with the faculty if possible.

5. Inform the students. The use of an assembly or public address system is not advised to announce a death.

6. Permit students to leave campus only with parental permission.

7. Provide counseling for friends and at-risk students. Some students will need to be seen individually; others may benefit more by sharing their thoughts and feelings in small groups. "At-risk" students refer to those who have experienced a recent loss or have threatened or attempted suicide.

8. Prepare a media statement and a fact sheet for telephone inquiries.

9. Send letters to elementary school parents about the death, how the school is responding, and what reactions might be expected from their child. Invite parents to contact the school counselor if they want assistance or have suggestions about how the counselor may help their child. (Make certain the letters are prepared in appropriate languages for non-English speaking families as needed.)

10. Appoint someone to coordinate memorials, cards, and contributions such as food for the family.

11. Inform students and staff about the funeral arrangements as soon as possible.

12. Request assistance from the district administration should substitutes be needed for teachers attending the funeral.

13. Debrief with the school crisis team.

14. Plan follow-up counseling for students and faculty as needed.

Declaration of War or Other Major National Incident (Level 2)

1. Verify information and gather details.

2. Share facts with the faculty via memo or meeting.

3. Discuss what happened with the students in small groups (e.g., a classroom) encouraging them to share their emotional reactions about the tragedy. Expect emotional reactions to vary with age and temperament.

4. Send letters to elementary school parents in appropriate languages. Describe what the school is doing and how the children may react. Include the phone numbers of the school for questions or for alerting the counselors about special problems children may have.

5. Hold an after-school faculty meeting to discuss how the students are responding and to clarify helpful approaches or further steps in dealing with the tragedy.

School Bus Accident with Injuries (Level 2)

1. Verify the report with the police department. Attempt to determine who has been injured, the extent of injuries, and the hospital(s) where students have been transported.

2. Prepare a list of the injured students' parents and emergency phone numbers. (The hospital may not have access to this information.)

3. Ensure that students with minor injuries are treated by the school nurse.

4. Notify the district administration.

5. Convene the local school crisis team. Ask some team members to meet at the hospital and other team members to assist at the school with friends and classmates of the injured.

6. Prepare a fact sheet for telephone inquiries.

7. Prepare a statement for the media.

8. Check about school insurance coverage or the school district's responsibilities for hospital expenses. Inform parents where the information may be found.

Suicide Attempt at School (Level 2)

1. Request the school nurse to administer first aid.

2. If the attempt is a medical emergency, call paramedics for transportation to a hospital emergency room. Have the school psychologist meet the parents there. Do not ask any school personnel who does not have special insurance coverage to transport a suicidal student to a hospital or home.

3. If an ambulance is not needed, ask the parents to come to the school to meet with the school psychologist.

4. Have crisis counseling provided for the suicidal student while awaiting the arrival of the parents or for transportation to a medical facility.

5. Clear witnesses from the area.

6. Help witnesses process their thoughts and feelings about what has happened.

7. Notify the district administration.

8. Formulate a re-entry plan with the parents, student, and appropriate staff to address the needs of the student when returning to school after an absence for hospitalization or treatment. If the student was treated at a hospital, a medical release should be required to return to school. If no medical assistance is needed, recommendations from the mental health professional who is counseling the student should be requested. Respect cultural differences or a desire for confidentiality by some parents.

Undercover Police Work Disclosed (Level 2)

1. Meet with the police to determine what information should be disclosed.

2. Call a faculty meeting. Instruct the teachers to give the students agreed-upon information.

3. Ask the crisis team counselors for recommendations to help angry or fearful students.

4. Prepare a statement for the media.

5. Prepare a fact sheet for telephone inquiries.

6. If parental response is strong, organize a parent meeting. Ask police, district administrators, and members of the crisis team to attend the meeting.

Level 3

Cluster Suicides (Level 3)

After Each Death (See suggested procedures for Death off Campus, Level 2)

1. Verify information from reporting source (family, witness, police, etc.)

2. Notify district administration.

3. Convene the local school crisis team.

4. Call a faculty meeting before school or inform staff by memo.

5. Inform students in the classrooms. Using a public address system to announce deaths or holding an assembly at this time is not recommended. Counselors, psychologists, and social workers may assist by visiting classrooms to discuss deaths as requested.

6. Prepare notes for the media.

7. Write a fact sheet for telephone inquiries.

8. Provide group counseling for grieving students and individual counseling for students known to be or have been suicidal.

9. Disseminate information about the funerals or memorials.

10. Determine the most effective communication methods to inform parents about the deaths, including expected emotional responses of children, what the school is doing, funeral arrangements, and an invitation to contact the school. Respect cultural differences and a preference for privacy by some parents.

11. Allow students who bring written permission from parents to attend the funeral.

12. Make home visits with a teacher, counselor, or crisis team member to extend condolences.

13. Debrief with the crisis team members. Plan a long-term response with parents and community leaders to address preventative measures.

14. Document all decisions and actions taken.

Community Involvement for Cluster Suicides

1. Form a coordinating committee of school and community leaders to organize a response plan.

2. Identify and contact community resources including representatives of the clergy, parent groups, emergency medical services, crisis centers, media, police, student councils, private and agency mental health professionals to assist in a community prevention effort.

3. Meet with parents and community representatives to share and discuss ideas to prevent additional suicides. Arrange small discussion groups.

4. Identify additional vulnerable students, provide crisis counseling, and refer especially troubled students to community resources for additional treatment.

Death at School: Natural, Accident, Homicide, or Suicide (Level 3)

1. Call 911 for emergency assistance.

2. Clear students from the area.

3. Notify the family of the deceased. Home visitation is recommended. Later, the school may wish to deliver sympathy notes, food, other donated items, or money.

4. Convene the local school crisis team. Send someone to the hospital (if the victim is transported) to meet with the family and friends who may congregate there.

5. Notify the district administration.

6. Alert counselors at other schools where siblings are enrolled.

7. Inform the staff and student body. Using the public address system or holding an assembly at this time to announce a death is not recommended. Memos may be sent to the teachers or crisis counselors may visit classrooms to convey the information.

8. Permit students to leave the campus only with parental permission. Check identification if concerned parents come to the school to remove elementary-school-age children. Release students only to the parent who has custody.

9. Provide counseling, paying particular attention to friends of the deceased and those students with recent losses or a history of suicide threats or attempts. Some students will need to be seen individually, others may benefit more by sharing in a group.

10. Give factual information to the media.

11. Prepare a fact sheet for telephone inquiries.

12. Determine the most effective method to inform parents about the death, what the school is doing, and the reactions they may expect from their child.

13. Hold a faculty meeting as soon as possible to process feelings and plan for the anticipated reactions of students.

14. Relay additional information (funeral arrangements, etc.) as it becomes available. Respect the traditions of various cultures when appropriate.

15. Students should be permitted to attend the funeral with written permission from their parents.

16. Request assistance from the district administration should additional adults be needed to help in classrooms during a funeral. Teachers should not be responsible for taking students to a funeral.

17. Prepare to hold a community meeting if necessary.

18. Debrief with the school crisis team.

19. Plan for follow-up counseling for students and staff.

20. Log all decisions and actions taken.

Environmental Hazard: Release of Hazardous Material, Spill or Leak of Toxic Substance (Level 3)

Exterior Release

1. Verify information.

2. Call 911 for emergency assistance. Ask for advice whether to evacuate or shelter in place.

3. Provide for emergency medical care.

4. Notify school security. Request assistance from the maintenance department.

5. Convene the local school crisis team.

6. Notify the district administration.

7. Request assistance in notifying other school facilities that may be affected.

8. Estimate the extent of injuries or potential physical danger with the school nurse and health services administrator.

9. Keep a list of hospitalized individuals and where evacuated persons are located.

10. Set up an incident command center with communication capabilities on site.

If Instructed by the Fire Department to Shelter in Place

If the school building is used as an evacuation site, the city and Red Cross may assist. When an environmental hazard creates unsafe conditions for students to return to their homes after school, parents must be notified to pick them up before they can be dismissed.

- Shut down main electrical power sources to close all ventilation sources.

- Turn off main gas supply.

- Close all exterior doors and windows.

- Provide portable hand-held cellular or walkie-talkie communication to control building zones.

- Set portable AM/FM radios to the designated emergency radio station for additional emergency information.

If Instructed by the Fire Department to Evacuate

The city will most likely determine the temporary shelter site. City buses may provide transportation or the principal may request school buses depending on prearrangements.

- Instruct the teachers to bring their class roll or attendance books.

- Determine the direction of the prevailing wind.

- Prepare special-needs students and personnel for evacuation.

- Evacuate the site using a crosswind route to avoid fumes.

- Make arrangements for organizing students with the supervisor of the shelter site (usually the nearest recreation center) before allowing students to leave the buses. A school administrator should remain in charge of the students.

- Prepare a fact sheet for parent and community inquiries.

- Prepare a statement for the media.

- Ask the media to help notify parents when and where children will be released.

- Set up a system to check the identification of parents. Release children only to a parent with legal custody.

- Debrief with the school crisis team.

- Make preparations for the crisis team to continue with follow-up services.

- Document all decisions and actions taken.

Interior Release

1. Verify information

2. Call 911 for emergency assistance. Ask for advice whether to evacuate or shelter in place. Have multiple copies of the building's floor plan available for the fire department.

3. Notify school security.

4. Provide for emergency medical care.

5. Move staff and students from the affected area.

6. Close up and secure the affected area.

7. Post warning signs at the entrance. The fire department will assist.

8. Convene the local school crisis team.

9. Estimate the extent of injuries or potential physical danger with the school nurse and health services administrator.

10. Keep lists of hospitalized persons and where students and staff have evacuated to.

11. Set up an incident command center with communication capability on site.

If Instructed by the Fire Department to Shelter on Site

- Shut down main electrical power sources to close the ventilation system.

- Turn off main gas supply.

- Close all exterior doors and windows.

- Provide portable hand-held cellular communication or walkie-talkies to control building zones.

- Set the portable AM/FM radios to designated emergency radio station for additional emergency information.

If Instructed by the Fire Department to Evacuate

The city will most likely determine the temporary shelter. City buses may provide transportation or the principal may request school buses depending on prearrangements.

- Instruct teachers to bring their class attendance or roll books.

- Determine the direction of the prevailing wind.

- Prepare special needs students and personnel for evacuation.

- Evacuate the site using a crosswind route to avoid fumes.

- Make arrangements for organizing students with the supervisor of the shelter site (usually the closest recreation center) before allowing students to leave the buses. A school administrator should remain in charge of the students.

- Prepare a fact sheet for parent and community inquiries.

- Prepare a statement for the media.

- Ask media to help notify parents when and where children will be released.

- Set up a system to check the identification of parents. Release children only to a parent with legal custody.

- Debrief with the crisis team.

■ Make preparations for the team to continue with follow-up services.

■ Document all decisions and actions taken.

Explosion, Fire, or Plane
Crash into Building (Level 3)

1. Sound the fire alarm and evacuate the building immediately. Instruct teachers to bring their roll books or class attendance.

2. Contact 911 for emergency services. Have multiple copies of the building's floor plan available for the fire department.

3. Extinguish the fire when it can be done safely.

4. Provide first aid.

5. Shut off HVAC and close exterior windows.

6. Alert school security.

7. Notify the district administration.

8. Convene the local school crisis team.

9. Assist emergency personnel in locating injured persons. Follow instructions of police and fire department personnel.

10. Set up an incident command center with communication capability on site.

11. If students need to be transported to a shelter site:

   ■ Make arrangements for organizing students with the supervisor at the site before allowing students to leave the buses. A school administrator should remain in charge of the students. The city may determine the evacuation site and provide transportation or school buses may be requested depending on pre-arrangements.

   ■ Prepare a fact sheet for parent and community inquiries.

   ■ Set up a system to check identification of parents. Release children only to a parent with legal custody.

12. Keep lists of hospitalized persons and the places where students are being evacuated to.

13. Keep students and staff away from the building until the area is declared safe.

14. When the building is safe for re-entry, follow the instructions of fire department personnel.

15. Prepare a statement for the media.

16. Ask for media assistance in notifying parents and disseminating information about procedures for releasing students.

17. Contact the general maintenance supervisor to repair the damaged area, erect barricades, deodorize, etc.

18. Determine a location for temporary classrooms and supplies when needed.

19. Debrief with the crisis team.

20. Document all decisions and actions taken.

Riot Developing from Community or Political Protest Activity (Level 3)

1. Identify the group and the purpose of the protest.

2. Notify school security.

3. Notify police.

4. Notify district administration. Determine if mediation is needed.

5. If the group is disruptive, warn members they are in violation of the law and subject to arrest. Ask them to discontinue their activity.

6. Do not allow disruptive persons to enter school property. If the protest group is already on the school premises, request that the members vacate immediately. Assign staff to all building entrances to prevent further disturbances inside the facilities.

7. Advise teacher to keep classroom doors closed and locked if possible.

8. Keep administrative offices locked; provide security measures for files and records.

9. Keep the faculty informed through memos, brief meetings, or through other campus communication systems.

10. Prepare a statement for the media.

11. Prepare for community meetings that may be needed to respond to the demands or problems identified by the protesters.

12. Refer to the school board policy for disciplinary action if students are involved in demonstrations and create or threaten to create a substantial disruption in classes or school sponsored activities. Try to allow students the opportunity to voice opinions or dissent where they can be heard and appropriately responded to by administrators inside the building.

13. Request immediate assistance of law enforcement.

14. Keep district administration informed.

15. Alert crisis team members to assume their responsibilities.

16. Provide first aid or assist paramedics if possible.

17. Once order has been restored, remain alert for further campus disruptions. Ask student leaders for input regarding controversial issues. Ask for community involvement in resolution of concerns leading to the riot. Communicate with probation officers if any involved students are on probation.

18. Document all activities and decisions.

Taking Hostages or Sniper Gunfire (Level 3)

1. Call 911 for emergency assistance.

2. Convene local school crisis team.

    - Assess the situation (weapons, number of students, location, closest exit).

    - Secure the school building. Keep all students away from the area. Lock all doors.

    - Attempt to reduce the number of hostages immediately. The FBI recommends this procedure even before law enforcement arrives.

    - Inform the staff through a code to keep all students in the classrooms and away from the windows. Hold the change-of-class bell.

    - Have multiple copies of the building's floor plan available for the police.

3. Set up an incident command center with communication capabilities on site.

4. Remain available to law enforcement and negotiators.

5. Confer with the district administration.

6. Have an attendance roster available to use as a checklist when releasing students. Ask teachers to remain with their students until the situation is resolved or students are released to their parents. Use prearranged evacuation site to release students to parents if necessary.

7. Prepare a statement for the media. Prohibit media access to students in the school building. This contact tends to be disruptive.

8. Prepare a fact sheet for phone calls from parents and the community.

9. Debrief with the school crisis team.

10. Make preparations for the school crisis team to provide follow-up services.

11. Document all decisions and actions taken.

Tornado, Severe Storm, or Flood (Level 3)

1. Contact emergency services, 911, and school security.

2. Convene the local school crisis team.

3. In case of a tornado warning, post trackers to observe.

4. Tune to a battery-powered radio for additional weather information.

5. If high-intensity winds are threatening, evacuate those classrooms bearing the full force of the wind immediately to a safe area within the building.

6. If a funnel cloud is sighted, move the staff and students to a safe area (inner hallways, inside wall on the bottom floor, or best available space away from windows). Do not shelter persons within the building in auditoriums, gymnasiums, or other room with large roof spans.

7. If the storm is accompanied by severe flooding, relocate students and staff to an area safe from flooding, relocate students and staff to an area safe from flooding until further instructions are received from the city fire department.

8. Prepare for additional emergency action such as medical triage in conjunction with police and fire department instructions.

9. Prepare special-needs students, all other students, and personnel for full evacuation. The city will most likely determine the evacuation site. City buses may provide transportation or the principal may request school buses depending on what has been prearranged.

    - Instruct the teachers to bring their class roll or attendance books.

    - Make arrangements for organizing students with the supervisor of the evacuation site (usually the nearest recreation center) before allowing students to leave the buses. A

117

school administrator should remain in charge of the students.

- Ask the media to help notify parents when and where children will be released.

- Set up a system to check the identification of parents. Release children only to a parent with legal custody.

10. Confer with the district administration.

11. Set up an incident command center with communication capability on site.

12. Keep a record of those persons who have been hospitalized or evacuated and where they have been taken.

13. Prepare a statement for the media.

14. Debrief with the local school crisis team and plan for follow-up services for students and staff.

15. Document all decisions and actions taken.

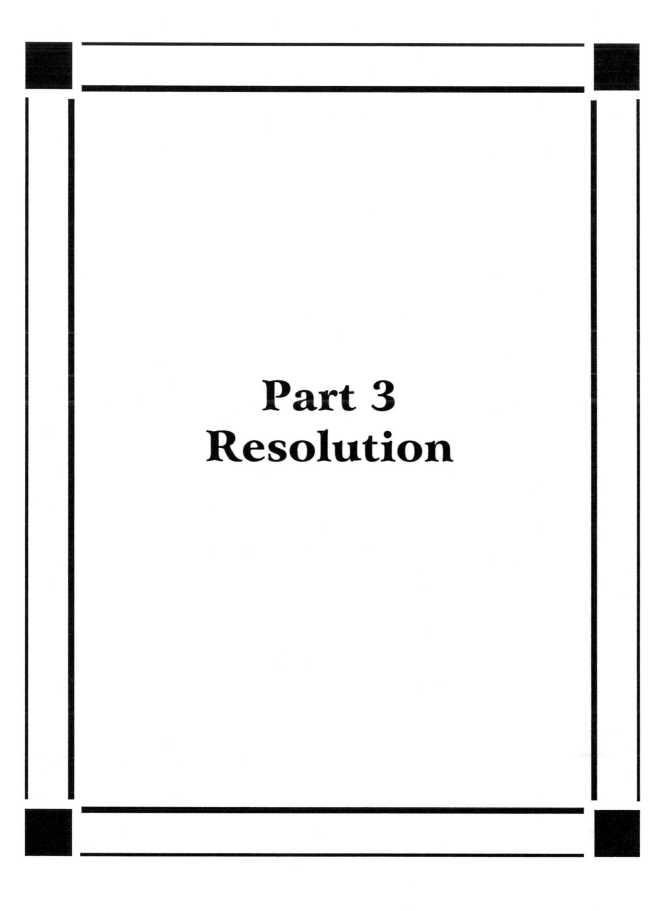

Part 3
Resolution

Grief and Loss

A personal crisis is usually precipitated by the loss of something or someone close. Schools need to be prepared to help students who are grieving and assist them through this life crisis. An informed professional can effectively use the school environment to offer understanding, stability, and support to a child in mourning. A few kind words acknowledging the loss when the student returns to the classroom, a home visit to extend condolences to the family, showing understanding when the child exhibits moodiness or anger, and expressing tolerance when assignments are turned in late are all helpful.

A student may misbehave and have classroom difficulties soon after the death of a family member or friend as he or she adjusts to the empty feeling and the changes in life that the death brings. Depending on the circumstances of the death and the relationship of the deceased, the feelings that smolder or surface can be bewildering to the young person as well as the teacher and classmates.

When death occurs to someone who is well-known in school and liked by many students and faculty, the crisis expands beyond the personal tragedy into a major concern for the school. If an illness is the cause of death there usually is some preparatory time to deal with the feelings. The shock is not as great as when the death occurs suddenly. Nonetheless, when the news reaches the school, the normal routine will be disrupted. The disruption may last for several days as people get used to being at school without the deceased. The school environment will feel strange. The death reminds people of other losses they may have suffered in the past and it brings old grief symptoms fresh again. There usually is a lot of conversation about the death because it is on everyone's mind.

There would be no preparatory time if the death were sudden and the emotional reaction may become overwhelming as students and teachers learn about it. It is important for the school to respond in a way to allow people the opportunity to begin mourning by learning all the circumstances surrounding the death and to express their feelings. The death story may have to be repeated over and over. This repetition helps people accept the reality of the loss. If information is withheld there is a tendency to fill in the blanks with imagination and rumor. No matter how horrendous the circumstances, rumor is worse than the truth.

On occasion a death may actually happen at school. A teacher may die from a heart attack, a child may choke in the cafeteria, a student may commit suicide in front of a class. These events cause a great deal of turmoil and chaos. People may assume undeserved responsibility and guilt because they think they could have prevented the death. For many it will be the first experience of witnessing death which can be very frightening. A violent homicide or suicide may trigger anger that will be difficult to contain. Crisis management procedures need to be planned prior to these possible events. Outside assistance is helpful. After the initial crisis has calmed down, ongoing support and follow-up counseling may be necessary for those who are most deeply affected.

Children are particularly vulnerable to the suffering that accompanies grief. They may respond differently from the typical mourning behavior of adults and thus their needs may not be recognized. They may have a sense of helplessness, confusion, fear, and sadness but these feelings aren't expressed in the same way as an adult. Children's understanding of death changes as they develop and their grief responses begin to imitate the traditional grief behavior of the adults in their family. Because a seven-year-old is observed playing in the yard outside a funeral home while his family mourns the death of his father inside does not mean the child is not affected by the death.

Unfortunately young child are sometimes removed from the family during the initial mourning phase to "protect" them from suffering. A child needs to learn how to cope with loss. This is best done within the warmth and love of the family circle. Children learn from other family members how to grieve and to help others who are grieving. Families are turning more and more to the schools for guidance with grieving children.

Children's Concept of Death

Children conceive of death differently from adults. It helps adults who are supporting and consoling a grieving child to realize that children's reaction to death depends on what they think causes death. As children mature with age their cognitive abilities increase and they become more logical and can understand how and why people die. Wilson (1988) has summarized these stages of children's concepts of death.

Ages 18 to 24 Months or Younger

Infants do not have concepts but do have intense subjective images. They do not fully understand that an object has no existence apart from their sensory perception of seeing, hearing, touching, or tasting. If a parent dies, they may become distressed at the absence of a caretaker but do not comprehend death.

Three to Five Years Old

Preschoolers think that dead people are not really dead but continue to live under changed circumstances. There are several systems of thinking about causes of death at this age:

1. Animistic thinking assumes that everything in the whole world is alive. Preschoolers believe inanimate objects can move, think, feel, and be at rest. Thus people too are always alive. Death is merely a deep sleep. Children worry about the comfort and physical care of dead bodies. They are concerned that the dead person might be hungry, cold, or lonely.

2. Magical thinking attributes a power to everyone. Everything is under the control of someone else's will. Within this system,

people can die because of another's wish and can return to life just as readily. A prince can turn into a toad and a dead princess can wake up with a kiss.

3. Artificialistic thinking is the belief that things exist for people's convenience. If toys can be fixed upon request, then why not dead people?

4. Personal motives are ascribed to certain events. Bad dreams are a punishment for misbehavior; bad falls are caused by eating too much candy. Wrong thoughts or deeds can also bring death.

Death is temporary, reversible, and caused magically. Children at this age tend to respond in varied, often contradictory, and unpredictable ways. They may be angry at the dead person for abandoning them or anxious that others might also leave them. A preschooler may be convinced that some thought or action of their own caused the death. Adults must be sensitive to changes in behavior driven by guilt feelings.

Six to Eight Years Old

Death is conceived as a person. If the child's magic is strong enough, death can be fought and mastered. Death does not take young and healthy people. Only the old and sick are too weak to hold death off. The dead can still see, hear, eat, and breathe. This causes many fears about the fate of the corpse. Children at this age may worry about being trapped in coffins. They are fascinated by what happens to corpses after death and may be preoccupied with decomposition and decay.

Nine to 12 Years Old

Children now know that what lives also dies. They have let go of the magical thinking and replace it with a higher order of logic. Death is understood as normal and irreversible. Dead people cannot be brought back to life. They are concrete and objective in their reasoning. They still may think death will not happen to them until

124

they are very old. In fact, with luck, it is possible to escape death altogether.

Children at this developmental stage understand internal illness as a cause of death as well as physical violence and accidents. Their anxieties are more likely to be related to the physical consequences of death than to separation. Physical causality is understood so their fears may focus on bodily mutilation, being buried alive, and on the physical process of death. Since they understand the irreversibility of death they may receive comfort from a belief of life after death but still have difficulty visualizing a decaying body in a coffin and in heaven at the same time. The concept of a soul is too abstract for an 11-year-old to understand.

Adolescence

Death is final and irreversible. It happens to everyone, including them. Adolescents are as capable of abstract reasoning as adults. They are concerned with theological beliefs or explanations of life after death. Death is remote and spiritual rather than concrete and physical. It is inevitable, but will not happen immediately. Adolescents live for the moment and they may deny the possibility that death could interrupt any of their current or life plans. Adolescents may take unwarranted risks when seeking thrills or impressing friends because they do not accept the reality of personal danger. They may focus on the glory of death and idolize a peer who dies.

Stages of Grief

The course of normal grief has similarities as well as differences. People grieve in their own way. Those in mourning must progress through the grief process, regardless how painful, if loss is to be resolved with time. Unfortunately, unresolved grief can manifest itself many years later. Individuals with unresolved grief pay a high price in mental distress and illness.

Kubler-Ross

Kubler-Ross (1969) is a pioneer in the field of thanatology. She studied the emotional process of death and dying and found a common progression of thinking and feelings people go through as they are dying. Loved ones of the dying person also go through similar stages.

1. The initial reaction is denial. It is hard to believe or accept the impending death.

2. The second stage is anger. "Why me?" The anger is directed at everybody.

3. Some people may then try to bargain to have the death put off. There are so many unfinished thing to do. Promises are made to God or whomever is perceived to have the power to prolong the inevitable.

4. Depression may follow when the realization sets in that death will be a reality. They are mourning for their own death and losses.

5. Finally, the dying person accepts what is happening and may withdraw from loved ones, reviews the past life with satisfaction and is ready for death with quiet resolution.

Westburg

Westburg (1962) believes that grief is a natural part of human experience. When grief strikes, it can panic someone who knows little about its nature. When people understand the grief process they can better cope with it. Grief applies to other losses as well as a loss from a death. When a family is uprooted and cut off from the established relationships in the former community, a child looses support and friendships of neighbors and peers. Divorce can affect children by creating feelings of insecurity and grief.

There are 10 stages of grief that people go through after a loss before they find their way back to the "mainstream of life." These grief experiences are normal but not everyone experiences them in the same order or necessarily goes through all the stages.

1. Shock
2. Expression of emotion
3. Depression and loneliness
4. Physical symptoms of distress
5. Panic

6. Sense of guilt
7. Anger and resentment
8. Resistance
9. Hope
10. Affirmation of reality

Tasks of Mourning

Grief has often been described as "grief work." It is not a passive process that will simply happen without effort or pain. To progress through the stages, a grieving person has to be active or, as Worden (1982) explains, has to accomplish certain tasks. To view mourning this way means taking advantage of opportunities and creating others that permit "working through" grief. Mourning is a long-term process. It is not over in six weeks or even six months.

Task 1. To accept the reality of loss. The shock of loss is great. There is a tendency to deny that the death occurred or deny the significance of the loss.

Task 2. To experience the pain of grief. The pain is both physical and emotional. It hurts. Avoidance and suppression of the pain prolongs the mourning process.

Task 3. To adjust to an environment in which the deceased is missing. Changes in the daily living routine happen

127

after a loss. Excessive dependency on others will foster helplessness.

Task 4. To withdraw emotional energy and reinvest in another relationship. Past attachment with the deceased is lessened without betraying the memory and new relationships are formed. The gap may be filled but it nevertheless remains something else. Life changes.

Strategies for Schools

The primary source of support for grieving children will be the home, but students and parents also look to the schools to provide additional resources and guidance. Based on the understanding of how children conceive death, the stages of grief, and the tasks of mourning, the following are some activities and strategies that schools can utilize.

1. Tell the children about the death with clear, honest information.

2. Correct any misconceptions.

3. Encourage children to express and share their feelings. Empathize with anger and reassure that it is part of grief.

4. Provide comfort.

5. Allow children to participate in memorials, funerals, or other ceremonies associated with the death. Prepare them for the experience by explaining what may happen.

6. Maintain consistency and predictability of the school routine.

7. Communicate with parents about the child's behavior relating to expressions of grief.

8. Encourage projects such as collecting writings, drawings, and pictures into a scrapbook of memories.

9. Help the children create and send sympathy cards.

128

10. Prepare classmates to receive a child, who may have experienced a significant loss, back to school.

11. Provide individual and group crisis counseling.

Post-Traumatic Stress

School administrators need to be aware that there are possible serious consequences of psychological trauma after exposure to severe and extraordinary stress. When the body has to adapt to demands from the environment, it is considered to be under stress. These demands for adaptations are called stressors. Stress in itself is neither good nor bad. A stressor can bring joy and pleasure as well as fright and anger. Stress keeps people from becoming stagnant, but with too much stress they can become overwhelmed. Involuntary patterns of feelings, thoughts, or behaviors arise in response to real or perceived danger. These patterns are called coping or defense mechanisms and serve the purpose of reducing the effects of stress. When ordinary coping and defenses are overwhelmed during a crisis, psychological trauma occurs.

Post-Traumatic Stress Disorder (PTSD) may develop when normal responses to abnormal and exceptionally severe stressors become exaggerated and protracted. Similar to bereavement, such responses to extreme stressors do not necessarily constitute a mental disorder. But when symptoms last up to three months it may be considered acute PTSD. Chronic PTSD lasts for more than three months. Or the onset of the PTSD symptoms may be delayed for several months after the exposure to the crisis when an individual encounters a circumstance similar to the original stressor that aggravates or rekindles the symptoms.

Either experiencing or witnessing a catastrophic event may result in post-traumatic stress if it is perceived as threatening. These events may include violence, disasters, accidents, or traumatic deaths.

- Violence: shootings, beatings, robberies, hostage situations, etc.

- Disaster: tornadoes, floods, hurricanes, earthquakes, etc.

- Accidents: automobile, explosions, airplane, burns, falls, etc.

- Traumatic deaths: suicide, murder, sudden heart attack or stroke, torture, or abuse, etc.

Immediate intense emotional reactions are normal consequences of an abnormal crisis event. When the reactions are prolonged they become a psychological disorder. Some manifestations of the disorder in children include:

- Repetitive play to relieve or gain mastery over the trauma.

- Diminished interest in activities or schoolwork and seems overwhelmed by everyday situations.

- Difficulty falling or staying asleep.

- Nightmares or recurrent distressing dreams of the event.

- Refusal to talk about the trauma. Efforts to avoid thoughts, feelings, activities, or play that arouse recollections of the trauma.

- Constriction of affect, appears to be "emotionally numb."

- Easily startled or increased arousal (hypervigilance).

- Lack of orientation toward the future or having a sense of doom about the future.

- Re-experiencing the event through disturbing intrusions of vivid images, thoughts, or sounds related to the trauma (flashbacks).

- Frequent crying.

- Irritability or outbursts of anger.

- Inability to recall an important aspect of the trauma.

- Difficulty concentrating.

Immediate psychological first aide and effective screening of students and staff exposed to a violent or traumatic event may prevent the development of Post-Traumatic Stress Disorder. If children are given the opportunity to face the reality of what has occurred, to ventilate thoughts and emotions, and to mourn with the care and support from adults, normal reactions to a crisis may not become abnormal and exaggerated reactions.

Screening by the crisis counselors identifies those who may need continuing support or treatment. Witnesses and victims would need immediate attention. Children who have been exposed to repeated violence or have had previous psychological trauma are particularly vulnerable and should also be referred to a counselor. These students need the opportunity to talk about their feelings and thoughts several days after the crisis and on a weekly basis until they have had a chance to "integrate the experience into their lives and restructure their beliefs about the world" (Peterson and Straub 1992). Parents need to be cautioned to stay alert for any continuing changes in their child's behavior that would include several of the above characteristics and to notify the school for assistance if they do appear.

People remember traumatic emotional events and, years later, may vividly recall what happened. Sometimes major life changes are made as a result of a crisis. Decisions may be made to take a different direction toward a career, an educational goal, or to devote time and energy to a particular cause. Children mature emotionally as they develop coping skills and defense mechanisms by surviving a personal crisis. A child's world of innocence is diminished when the bubble of protection is punctured and the realities of danger and loss are experienced. We wish crises never would have to happen, particularly at school without the nurturing of the family present. But if children are given the opportunity to express and process their reactions, they are much more likely to grow from a crisis experience instead of develop distressful symptoms of post-traumatic stress.

Crisis Counseling

Resolution will not come from being told to put a traumatic event aside and forget it. The emotional impact of a crisis makes the experience indelible. The stronger the fear, anger, or grief, the stronger the memory. Witnessing the death of a classmate, huddling in a hallway to escape the fury of a tornado, or watching little children run to escape gunfire on the playground is likely to create memories that will remain long after the danger has passed. Resolution comes when these events are remembered and talked about without bringing up the sharp fear, anger, or grief feelings and the memories do not interfere with the normal productive activity and requirements of the day. Most children are resilient and do survive school crises without lasting emotional or behavior problems.

Just as the key to effective crisis management is communication, the key to emotional resolution after a crisis is counseling. One of the goals of crisis management is to return the school to its normal routine as soon as possible. Providing immediate crisis counseling is the means to achieve this goal and to help prevent long-lasting problems of post-traumatic stress. Counseling should be made available to help the students and staff deal with their emotions and begin the healing process. The quicker the crisis counselors can mobilize the better.

The principal and the crisis specialist or the school psychologist can decide together how many crisis counselors may be needed from the nature of the crisis event and estimated impact it will have on the school. It is better to have extra counselors in the beginning when the school first learns about the crisis. The team can be reduced as the initial reactions subside and only close friends or witnesses may need further counseling.

The typical reaction after exposure to a traumatic event is shock and numbness. Then comes the emotional reaction. School officials may hope all of this would happen after school is out for the day and some have been known to try to withhold news of a death to keep things quiet. But news travels quickly and rumors spread. It is very difficult to prevent the students from finding out. It is better to hear accurate information from teachers than half-truths from other students.

Once the group and individual counseling rooms are organized and the counselors in place, classroom activities need to be put aside to inform everyone what has happened as spelled out in the school's crisis plan. Those who become upset then need to be offered support from crisis counselors. Getting students to counseling sessions may actually seem to add to the chaos as young people seem to have a tendency to wander the halls or want to go home when they are upset, but they will be able to return to the classroom lessons sooner after dealing with their feelings with the help of a mental health professional.

Crisis counseling is a unique specialization that has emerged from a recognition that individuals have a better capacity to resolve their problems and deal with trauma when they have an opportunity to receive empathetic support. Empathetic support identifies what they are feeling and conveys acceptance of those feelings. Crisis counselors follow a crisis counseling model and are experts at "active listening."

The majority of school crises will involve a death or loss. Grief counseling is also a specialized counseling technique and involves careful strategies. Crisis counselors need training in children's' understanding of death, stages of grief, and tasks of mourning.

Crisis counseling can be conducted informally during a lunch period in the teachers' lounge or in a more structured atmosphere where chairs are placed in a circle in the home economics living room. Or a member of the crisis team may search for grieving students in the restroom or hanging out in the coach's office. Crisis counseling can happen in the corridor of a hospital or following a funeral service. The important thing to remember is to plan for it and to give permission for teachers and students to take advantage of it.

Conducting Crisis Counseling in the Classroom

Teachers may be asked to inform their students and lead discussions dealing with the crisis situation. The information may be given to the teachers by a telephone tree, at a faculty meeting, or by a memo from the principal. A member of the crisis team may be requested to assist a teacher as the news is relayed. If a student or teacher has died or is a victim of a serious and frightening crime, a member of the crisis team may need to follow the victim's class schedule throughout the day to inform and provide counseling to classmates.

Announcements over the public address system into each classroom should not be made until the students and faculty already know what has happened. No one should learn of the tragedy or loss from a loud speaker. Large assemblies encourage hysteria and do not allow the opportunity to process feelings or ask questions. Classroom visits permit valuable small group discussions.

The teacher or a familiar person should give the information initially. It is easier for students to accept the reality if the information is heard from someone they know. The crisis counselor can pitch in after the initial information is given.

If the teacher does not wish to inform the class, the crisis counselor may prepare the students for something unpleasant to come by saying he or she is going to tell them something very sad. If some of the students already know about it they should be asked to tell the rest of the class what they witnessed or were told. Errors need to be corrected. The counselor states the source of the facts (family, police, or other authorities) and reveals everything that is known except any gory or horrifying details.

Possible emotional reactions are acknowledged. The counselor needs to be prepared with lots of tissues. It is all right for the teacher to weep in front of the students and they are reassured that tears are okay for them too. Sometimes the teacher will not be comfortable letting the class see his or her tears and will leave the room. Students are not removed from the classroom unless they are not able to continue with the class after the visit. Individual or group counseling is arranged for distraught students. When one begins to cry it may spark the others to cry also.

The counselor anticipates fears and emphasizes feelings refraining from taking the opportunity to lecture on subjects such as the danger of gangs, drugs, guns, and traffic, or moralize about topics such as suicide, AIDS, criminal behavior, and sex. If students seem to focus on their fears, the counselor may ask what they could do to keep themselves safe.

Questions are encouraged. Students may ask for more details about the sequence of events including when, where, and how. Assumptions are not made unless they are labeled as what is thought but not necessarily known.

Most children will be reminded of other personal tragedies, incidents of violence, or deaths in their own families. The class may be asked if they have known anyone to die, seriously hurt in an accident, shot, etc. More time will be needed leading this kind of discussion than on the crisis event itself.

The students may point out which desk belonged to the deceased classmate. The class needs to decide what to do with it. The desk could remain empty, children could take turns sitting in it, it could be removed from the room, or reassigned to another student. Sometimes the class decides to decorate the desk or locker door with flowers, ribbons, and poems as a memorial. If the desk is ignored it can become a "ghost." The family may choose to gather other personal belongings in the locker or classroom assignments at a private time or may ask the teacher to put everything together to be delivered to the home.

Memories are encouraged of the deceased or victim. Children are asked to describe him or her; what she looked like, what were his favorite things to do. This storytelling brings up happy memories of what fun times they had together or something special that was said as well as sad memories. The mood of the class may lift with smiles when they talk of good times together.

The students need to be prepared for a funeral experience. Those who have attended one can describe the experience. Sometimes students will want to know if the casket will be open or will they have to watch the coffin be lowered into the ground. Children are encouraged to attend the funeral with their parents. Teachers should not be responsible for taking or supervising their students at a funeral. They will need the opportunity to do their own personal grieving.

Children who are most affected by the situation — a previous victim, witness, close friend, or a child who may have a family illness or recent death — should be identified and included in a support group session or given individual counseling instead of staying in the classroom during a visit from the crisis team.

Young children can draw or write sympathy cards. They may be addressed to the family but sometimes a child will want to write a note to the deceased. Students need to be encouraged with the project but their privacy should be respected if they do not wish to share the note. Sometimes the class will choose to write cards in a group project. One student will draw the cover, one will write on the board what the class wants to say, one will copy the words from the board onto the card, etc. Often students will compose poems. These activities facilitate their expression of feelings, helps give mastery over thoughts and is usually deeply appreciated by the family. Sometimes the family will even place the cards in the coffin.

All messages and pictures need to be screened before being delivered to the family. Even though it is cathartic, sometimes the children's fears and anger is expressed inappropriately for the family to read. The time necessary to cover these points will vary with the age of the children and the nature of the event.

The classroom visit may not follow a death but something else frightening such as witnessing an accident. One very productive classroom visit followed the loss of all personal belongings and class projects after plants along a windowsill were sprayed by the teacher with a strong insecticide that entered the school ventilation system. The school building was evacuated to the outside portable buildings, the room decontaminated and repainted by a hazardous material spill team, and the teacher almost lost her job.

A crisis counselor led the fifth grade students in a discussion the following morning of what they saw when the fire trucks came and the ambulance took some rescue workers to the hospital. The children also laughed about a truck getting stuck in the mud and men decked out in what looked like space suits waddling into the building. They eventually smiled over the 800 donated hamburgers and using the across-the-street neighbors' bathrooms. At first they were sad to loose their bookbags and a special project they had worked on. The discussion turned toward the normality of making mistakes and what you do after you have done something wrong. The teacher had not entered into the discussion until this point. Then, in a touching scene, she accepted responsibility for their loss with tears and asked for their forgiveness. The students gathered around her with hugs and expressions of total acceptance. It was a powerful experience for the children, the teacher, and the crisis counselor.

Grief Support Group Counseling

A major strategy of schoolwide crisis management is offering students an opportunity to deal with their emotional responses to the crisis situation in a group counseling setting. No written permission from parents is required for crisis counseling but if the group continues longer than two or three sessions the parents should sign a permission slip.

The ideal group size is eight to 10. Two facilitators work well for larger groups. Groups are recommended so the participants can support each other and understand that they aren't the only ones who are having such difficulty with their loss. If a student is not ready for a group experience because of suicidal behavior or other sensitive problems, he or she should be seen individually.

A screening procedure should be set up to triage students into the appropriate group. Closest friends could compose one group, acquaintances and classmates another. One close friend or a member of the family can usually identify others who may with to join the group. Sometimes kids may not be suffering as much as the others and will be taking advantage of an opportunity to get out of class. Others in the group may resent their inclusion. Students who may have conflicts with each other can be assigned separate groups. A grief group was once hastily formed after the homicide of a tenth grade student. Unbeknownst to the facilitator, the current girlfriend and the victim's former girlfriend, who happened to be the mother of his child, were assigned to the same group. Once the mistake was apparent, the girls were quickly reassigned to separate groups.

The arrangement of furniture and the room itself can hinder or facilitate group work. The chairs are placed in a circle without a table or barrier in the middle. If students sit on top of desks or on the floor all need to have eye contact with each other and the facilitators. The auditorium or cafeteria is too large, public, and noisy. A home economics living room, conference room, or office will provide a more comfortable atmosphere.

Getting started can be difficult if the students are uncomfortable, do not wish to speak up, or if they cry uncontrollably. An abundance of tissues should be scattered around. It may be necessary for the crying and hugging to continue for some time. This is an important part of the beginning of the grief process. If another student joins the group after the rest have calmed down, the tears may resume. Touching and hugging among the students is soothing but the facilitator should ask permission before offering more than a pat on the shoulder or gentle touch on the arm.

The facilitator can get the group going with a self-introduction, state the purpose of the group, and acknowledge their need to be together. The group is a place to talk about what has happened and their feelings about it. The students will be asked to respect confidentiality and not repeat what is shared to others outside the group. The facilitator agrees to the same confidentiality unless a student threatens suicide, homicide, or reveals child abuse.

The first task of mourning is to accept the reality of the loss. Students are asked what they know about what has happened that they are willing to share. Many times the student grapevine has more information than the police. Sometimes the story gets embellished and facts become twisted. Misinformation needs to be corrected to eliminate rumors. Little things may be important to friends, for instance, the exact time of death, who else was involved in the accident, or the make of the gun. Assumptions are separated from what is actually known as factual. Speculation may be dangerous such as identifying a gang as responsible. Students are encouraged to repeat where they were when they first learned about the death or tragedy and how it was told to them. These stories need to be repeated over and over for the reality to sink in.

The goal of grief crisis counseling is not to take away the sadness and pain but to facilitate the experiencing of the sadness and pain. Active listening is the major counseling technique to facilitate this. People grieve in different ways and these individual differences should be accepted. It is not as important how the feelings are expressed as it is to experience them. Each group member is encouraged to talk but any desire to remain attentive but silent is respected. Students may be asked to talk about the last time they saw the deceased, where they were, and what was said. Often the friends are experiencing regret that they did not have a chance to say goodbye. If this is an important issue they can be encouraged to find a time or way to express their thoughts to the deceased perhaps at the cemetery, during a wake, or in a letter. The group facilitator may ask these students to think of what they wish they would have said to their friend if they knew they wouldn't see him or her alive again.

Grieving is more difficult if there has been a recent disagreement between a friend and the deceased. Problems that are brought out in the group discussion are not judged. Finding a way to apologize is similar to saying goodbye. Most grieving people will find relief after they have done this symbolically.

Grief may cause physical problems and disruption of the daily routine. Students need to be informed to anticipate difficulty in sleeping, possibly with nightmares, or eating, and the importance of taking care of themselves with plenty or rest and exercise. Hearing or seeing visions of the deceased during acute grief does not indicate mental illness. This simply means the mind does not want to believe the friend is actually gone. A person in the crowd may look like the friend or his presence may be felt in a familiar room. It may be a frightening or a comforting experience.

Recalling memories — both happy and sad — are encouraged. Sometimes talking about happy times together will change the whole mood of the group. Tears will turn into smiles.

The group should be prepared for the funeral or the funeral may be described if it has already occurred. This discussion often brings memories of other loved ones who have died. The sharpness of fresh grief may reappear for someone who was close and died many years before. Time needs to be allowed for talking about other losses.

At times students may wish to wander in and out of the group. This can be difficult to control. However, it is important to keep the grieving students from disrupting the rest of the school. Assistance is sometimes necessary to escort them back to class. When the discussion strays to other topics it is an indication that the group is ready to dissolve. There still may be students who are not able to go back to class for the rest of the day. A parent should be contacted to take the student home. It is not prudent to allow a student to go home alone to an empty house. Closure can be brought to the group by summarizing with a review of feelings and any information about the funeral. The group can then decide if they want an opportunity to meet again.

Miscellaneous Strategies

Crisis team members may be asked to help a school "family" recover from a major crisis by working with the staff informally, visiting parents and siblings, or assisting students who are sent to the hospital. When someone trained in crisis counseling reaches out to those affected, it will facilitate the emotional healing. It helps to face a difficult situation knowing more what to expect and having someone there to listen and comfort. The contact offers an opportunity for the family and friends to process the experience and understand their own reactions.

Informal Contact with Staff

Teachers and support staff are also affected when a crisis occurs in a school and may need an opportunity to sort out and deal with their own reactions. The crisis team may offer to facilitate a support group after school but another effective strategy is for the crisis counselors to be available in the teachers' lounge or cafeteria during planning periods and lunch break. The conversation will focus on the crisis event wherever the teachers congregate.

The objectives are similar to those for a support group. Misinformation is corrected, questions are asked how their students are doing, and their feelings are empathetically listened to. The crisis event can trigger emotions that have nothing to do with the present situation but to something that happened in their personal lives. Occasionally a vulnerable teacher may need an afternoon off to rest and recover.

Hospital Visits

Crisis intervention counseling can be offered in the halls, waiting areas, or in a hospital room. Students may need someone to help them process the traumatic experience of being injured or seriously ill. Students need someone with them from school until a parent arrives. Parents may need assistance with a complicated hospital procedure. Care must be taken not to interfere with an often hectic hospital routine or intrude when the family prefers privacy. Usually the hospital staff welcomes assistance from a school representative.

An injured student is encouraged to talk about what happened. He or she may wish to describe the details over and over again. Feelings are identified such as shock, fear, confusion, anger, and anxiety. Sometimes a student will worry about a missing belonging such as a book bag or purse. Sometimes he will worry about how much class time and school work will be missed. They should be reassured that taking care of their physical needs right now comes first and school work will fall into place in due time.

Families may ask about the financial responsibility if the injury occurred at school or at a school-related activity. No assurance should be given about any school financial assistance with the bills even if it was a school bus accident. The hospital will help the family file insurance claims.

The principal needs to be kept informed on the student's medical status and progress. The hospital will probably not release any information except through the family. A hospital visit will initiate this contact as well as offer support to the family. Sometimes a group of friends will be camping out in the waiting rooms and the crisis team can spend time listening to their concerns, what they have to say about what has happened, and particularly how they feel about it.

Faculty Meeting

When at all possible, a meeting should be called by the principal before the beginning of school to inform the teachers of the crisis, help them anticipate the students' reaction, and outline the services that will be available by the crisis team throughout the day. The teachers themselves probably will be affected and a meeting before classes begin will give them a moment to deal with their own emotions. Sometimes a meeting is held at the close of the school day to talk about the crisis (if it occurred during the day) and to see what the teachers might need. It also gives the faculty an opportunity to plan a memorial, to organize the collection of food, money, or send flowers to the family.

A crisis specialist may be called on to speak to the teachers about children's grief reactions. Younger children do not understand the finality of death and will expect a classmate to return. Older children may need help understanding what happens at a funeral or how to deal with the anger that the tragedy evoked in them. Most children are sensitive to the feelings displayed by adults. Talking about what has happened helps relieve the anxiety that may be aroused by what they are observing in others. Fears are generated when children are injured. The persistent thought that it may happen to them or another friend should be identified by a teacher or team member and steps need to be taken to assure protection and safety.

A printed fact sheet is helpful so teachers can talk to their class and not make errors in repeating the information. If any of the teachers are uncomfortable discussing the crisis situation with their students, a crisis member may offer to assist.

Home Visits

A visit to the home following the death of a student by a representative of the school honors the family. The principal needs to know the community and advise when it is appropriate to make this visit. A crisis team member and perhaps the teacher may accompany the principal on this visit. Sympathy cards made by the students may be delivered at this time. The principal can offer to bring the student's personal belongings or plan a private time for the parents or family members to collect them at school.

The purpose of a home visit is to offer condolences and to acknowledge the pain of losing a child. Parents may want to go over the events or illness that led to the death. They may want the school to know the details. Repeating the story also helps them accept that it really happened. This is the first task of mourning and, as painful as it might be, talking about it does serve a purpose. A parent may ask for a counselor to spend time with a sibling after returning to school or want messages taken back to the teacher and classmates.

Funerals

The school needs to be represented at a funeral. School is an important part of a child's life and the family appreciates the school's presence at this occasion. The principal may serve as the official representative and, depending on cultural traditions, may be expected to speak during the service.

A crisis team member may attend also but the purpose would be to see how the students are doing and talk to the teachers. The crisis counselor is not as involved emotionally and is there to support those who are. Students should be encouraged to attend with their parents to help them through a very emotional experience. The funeral serves the purpose of creating a setting for expression of grief and saying goodbye to the deceased. It facilitates acceptance of the reality of death to see the casket and hear a eulogy.

Community Meeting

A major crisis at a school is likely to arouse community reaction. The school is an extension of the community and a contributing part of the wholeness and vitality of the neighborhood. The current thrust in education is to encourage the community to become a stakeholder and increase its involvement in school activities to a greater extent than it has in the past. A crisis involving the school or the neighborhood children is a catalyst for bringing parents, ministers, political activists, and other community leaders to the school for answers and action. They may demand reassurance from the school administrators that the actions taken on the part of the school before, during, and after the crisis were appropriate and professional. A community meeting organized by the school administration is a primary vehicle for this reassurance. It is an excellent opportunity for team building and pulling together a web of community support.

A community meeting also presents a challenge. Much planning should be given to the organization and conducting of a gathering where emotions are likely to be intense. It should not become a political forum where activists or candidates seize the podium for votes or causes only loosely related to the crisis event. The media coverage unfortunately can encourage this to happen. Administrators need to keep the topic focused on the agenda issues and above all let everyone in attendance, who wishes to, speak. A test of strong leadership ability will be to accept all ideas and answer all questions without becoming defensive.

The difficulty lies in structuring the time where expression of anger or mistrust does not become contagious and the meeting turns into an unproductive evening of shouts and threats while little else is accomplished. Another challenge is to prevent a few

147

outspoken people from dominating the time resulting in parents leaving the meeting feeling uneasy and unsatisfied that the school is neither caring for the safety nor the education of their children.

First, the community should feel welcome. Have sufficient staff or volunteers present to greet people as they arrive, give directions to the meeting room, and hand out a printed agenda.

The principal will lead the meeting with support from other district administrators as is appropriate depending on the crisis. If a teacher has been accused of molesting children, bring someone from the personnel department who can explain district policy and state law on child abuse. If a student has been killed on campus, bring the director of the security department or police gang unit. Include the school crisis team.

After introductions have been made, the principal should state the purpose of the meeting and review any crisis details allowed by police without jeopardizing an investigation. Many times stories about the event have been generated from misinformed people and seem to take a life of their own. This meeting becomes an opportunity to give out correct and consistent information. A description of specific actions taken during the crisis on the part of the school and what is being planned for follow-up should also be included in this general session of the community meeting. Resist taking too many questions from the floor during this general session and try to focus the questions only on the information just given. Explain there will be plenty of opportunity for questions during the break-out sessions.

After the specific information has been given in the general session, break the meeting up into small discussion groups. Smaller groups of 15 to 20 participants is an important strategy to allow everyone to express ideas, complaints, and emotions. A discussion facilitator may be a member of the crisis team or an administrator who was involved in the managing of the crisis. Ask the group to appoint a recorder and a spokesperson.

The small group facilitator leads the group from positive aspects of the school's response to areas of concern. The sequence of discussion items may be as follows:

- As a result of the crisis at Horace Mann this week, what positive things do you see happening? What particularly pleased you about the way the school handled the crisis?

- What relationship is there between what happened at school and what goes on in the community?

- What concerns do you have about safety issues in your school?

- What possible solutions are there to those identified problems?

- What resources are available in the community to support the school's effort to provide a safe and secure learning environment for our students?

- How can communications between the school, parents, and the community be improved?

- Other concerns.

The recorder then reads the comments back to the group to be certain that everyone's concerns have been heard and recorded correctly. If time runs out before everyone has the opportunity to speak or any of the participants prefer not to speak openly, have cards available for them to write their concerns. Collect them and make sure an answer is given back to them in writing.

Reconvene the smaller groups back into the general session and ask a spokesperson from each group to report the highlights of their discussion emphasizing the possible solutions to their concerns. Summarize and thank the participants for attending.

Horace Mann High School
Community Meeting

Tuesday, January 19   7:00 p.m.   Auditorium

Let's Talk

Security   Instruction   Support

All parents and community members are invited to attend a community meeting. We will discuss ways to make Horace Mann even better, safer, and more successful in educating young people.

Crisis Summary Report

School _____ Date _____

Name(s) _____

_____

Grade(s) _____

Crisis Event _____

_____

_____

_____

Check Interventions

❑ Verify information from police
❑ Facilitate staff meeting
❑ Visit classes
❑ Group counseling of students
❑ Individual counseling of staff
❑ Group counseling of staff
❑ Hospital visit
❑ Individual counseling of students

❑ Make home visits
❑ Contact community agency
❑ Attend funeral or memorial
❑ Contact another school
❑ Meet with parents
❑ Community meeting
❑ Contact media

Other _____

Number of Students Seen Individually _____

Number of Students Seen in Group _____

Number of Classes Visited _____

Names of Students Needing Follow-Up Counseling

_____   _____

_____   _____

_____   _____

_____   _____

_____   _____

Names of Crisis Team Staff

_____   _____

_____   _____

_____   _____

_____   _____

Total Number of Staff _____   Total Staff Hours _____

Report Filed by _____

Date _____

Debriefing

Suggestions for Debriefing the Crisis Team

Debriefing during and after a crisis event allows the crisis team to process experiences. The purpose is not so much to gather information or interrogate as in the military sense, but to be able to vent feelings, bolster morale, prevent burn-out, and foster teamwork. The debriefing is a team process and an opportunity to learn from the experience.

1. Set a short debriefing session at the end of each day and a final one for when the crisis seems to be resolved. A crisis situation is most intense soon after the event or when people first learn about it. A meeting may need to be called midday on the first day. Having lunch together would be a good time to relax a little and do some sharing.

2. Give each participant an opportunity to describe their experiences of the day. What was the role of each in containing and resolving the crisis?

3. Allow stories to be told of personal tragedy and grief. Repeating the stories helps crisis workers deal with the trauma. Remember, the crisis team members will also be impacted by what is seen, heard, and felt.

4. Explore what team members need from each other to make their jobs go more smoothly.

5. Review what went particularly well. Compliment, stroke, praise. Crisis work is a strain on the team members. People will be tired. Acknowledge their efforts and thank them.

6. Decide where the problem areas were and how they can be corrected now or avoided in the future. Team members' responsibilities may need to be changed or the crisis plan itself revised based on this new information.

7. Provide for follow-up services for those affected the most. Traumatic experiences can result in post-traumatic stress or have a continuing influence on a child's vulnerability to psychological problems.

Stress Management Care for the Caregivers

No matter how much training or experience a crisis worker has, there is a tremendous amount of stress generated simply by helping others who are personally affected by a traumatic event. Stress can be defined as the body's emotional and physical reactions to a stressor. Tension, fatigue, anxiety, inability to concentrate, loss of appetite, and disturbances of sleep are some of the symptoms when an individual is reacting to stress. The stressor in this case for a crisis worker is the emotional outpouring and chaos that follows the wake of a school crisis.

The crisis team has a certain amount of objectivity because they are not directly acquainted or related to the victim(s). This objectivity aids them in being able to withstand or hold up to the bombardment of shock, despair, or grief that may be displayed by those more directly involved. However, everyone reacts with a certain amount of empathy by picturing themselves in the place of the victim or a friend of the victim. Empathy enables the crisis worker to be more effective because of the sincerity. If a sense of sincerity is missing by those needing relief, the crisis counseling will be empty and not well accepted.

A principal or school administrator may not be able to remain as objective due to the leadership role. He or she may feel responsible for not preventing the crisis. Or perhaps the principal doesn't want the community to know that a crisis has happened that may tarnish the image of the school. The team, through consultation and personal support, may also help administrators deal with the stress and consequently be in a better emotional position to make critical decisions.

Crisis workers and school counselors should always have permission to remove themselves from a crisis team if they are too close to the victim, witnessed the crisis event, or have other major stressors in their personal lives.

Beginning signs of burn-out for crisis counselors may include:

- Feeling apathetic, sad, anxious, guilty, helpless, or that it just doesn't matter any more.

- Being physically tired, nervous, having trouble sleeping, headaches, stomach pains, loss of appetite.

- Having difficulty concentrating or making decisions, easily distracted, confused.

Some specific suggestions that school administrators can do to support team members are:

- Provide refreshments, ice water, or other small comforts.

- Encourage them to take small breaks throughout the day and designate a space for the team to meet and relax.

- Participate in the debriefing sessions.

- Allow compensatory time for after-hours work.

- Recognize the team's contribution both verbally and in writing to the team members' supervisors.

The team will learn to reach out to each other and utilize their normal resources for stress management after working several crises together. Talking through their own experiences with someone who is willing and knows how to listen brings relief for them as well as those whom they may have just counseled. Often professional supervision is available for school mental health workers and stress management topics become an integral part of the supervision. The coordinator of the team needs to recognize the stress reactions of the members and assign the responsibilities accordingly. Sometimes it is necessary to be quite insistent, and at the same time respectful of a crisis counselor's own wishes, that it is time to take a break or bring in a partner to co-lead a group.

At the end of the school day a crisis counselor must learn to put the day's events aside and return to their own family and personal lives. Some individuals will treat themselves by scheduling a massage, jogging or working out, watching a good movie or reading a book, eating out or even just going shopping.

Helping a school recover from a crisis is a rewarding experience for all those involved in crisis management. The personal satisfaction of seeing the difference in the students and faculty after an intensive day of handling and resolving crisis makes the stress more tolerable.

REFERENCES

Crisis Management Plan Emergency Handbook. Dallas: Dallas Public Schools, 1992.

Crisis Management Plan for Schools. Houston: Berra Engineering, 1995.

Crisis Management Plan Resourse Manual. Dallas: Dallas Public Schools, 1992.

Doka, K. *Living with Grief after Sudden Loss.* Washington, D.C.: Hospice Foundation, 1996.

Dunne, E., J. McIntosh, and K. Dunne-Maxim. *Suicide and Its Aftermath: Understanding and Counseling the Survivors.* New York: Norton, 1987.

Grollman, E. *Explaining Death to Children.* Boston: Beacon Press, 1967.

Jewett, C. *Helping Children Cope with Separation and Loss.* Boston: Harvard Common Press, 1982.

Kubler-Ross, Elizabeth. *On Death and Dying.* New York: MacMillan, 1969.

"Mini-Series: School Violence." *School Psychology Review* 23, no. 2 (1994): 139-263.

Mitchell, J., and G. Bray. *Emergency Services Stress: Guidelines for Preserving the Health and Careers of Emergency Services Personnel.* Englewood Cliffs, N.J.: Prentice Hall, 1990.

Papadatos, D., and C. Papadatos. *Children and Death.* New York: Nemisphere, 1991.

Peiss, D., J. Richters, M. Radke-Yarrow, and D. Scharff. *Children and Violence.* New York: Guilford, 1993.

Petersen, S., and R. Straub. *School Crisis Survival Guide.* West Nyack, N.J.: Center for Applied Research in Education, 1992.

Poland, S., and G. Pitcher. *Crisis Intervention in the Schools.* New York: Guilford Press, 1992.

Puryear, D. *Helping People in Crisis.* San Fransisco: Jossey-Bass, 1979.

Safe Schools and Communities Satellite Seminar Series. Seminar 2: "Crisis Management and Intervention." St. Rose, LA: National TeleLearning Network, 1994.

School Safety Check Book. National School Safety Center. Malibu, CA.: Peperdine University Press, 1988.

Webb, N. *Helping Bereaved Children.* New York: Guilford, 1993.

Westburg, G. *Good Grief.* Philadelphia: Fortress, 1962.

Wheeler, E., and A. Baron. *Violence in Our Schools, Hospitals, and Public Places.* Ventura, CA: Pathfinder, 1994.

Wilson, P. "Helping Children Cope with Death," in *Crisis Counseling, Intervention, and Prevention in the Schools,* edited by C. Sandoval. Hillsdale, N.J.: Lawrence Erlbaum, 1988.

Worden, W. *Grief Counseling and Grief Therapy.* New York: Springer, 1982.